#myvoice

Vol. 6

#myvoice

Vol. 6

Inspiring Journeys of Self-Realisation, Perseverance & Fulfilment

GLOBAL INFLUENCERS

GLOBAL INFLUENCERS PUBLISHING HOUSE
152 Prince Charles Cr, #17-12 Singapore 159013
Website: www.globalinfluencers.sg
Email: shikha@globalinfluencers.sg
First Published in Singapore by
Global Influencers Publishing House 2023

Title: #myvoice Vol.6 - Inspiring Journeys of Self-Realisation, Perseverance & Fulfilment
ISBN: 978-981-18-6514-5

GLOBAL INFLUENCERS PUBLISHING HOUSE

Printed and bound by Redflame Publishers

Contents

Preface

"Put your oxygen mask on before assisting others."

#MyVoice Vol.6 – Inspiring Journeys of Self-Realisation, Perseverance & Fulfilment, is the latest volume in a series of ensemble volumes that highlights and celebrates the achievements and lives of twenty women from various backgrounds worldwide.

It should come as no surprise that there is discussion on an individual's different voices and how we come across them. Each of them is unique and wields a different power in the world.

We have the unusual stories of traditional islanders who seek and find new passion. They set their goals, articulate them and then pursue them until it is achieved — masterclass in perseverance for us all to follow.

There are stories of resilience through incredible hardship that would stop many people in their tracks instead of driving them to find a way to help others in the same situation. The outcomes are a win for the authors and all the women who benefit from reading their stories.

What happens when your world is literally shaken apart? The answer is that unexpected synergies occur between people who would not typically work together to achieve greatness in unforeseen ways. These are the insights into a genuine change in the direction of success for these women's lives.

The question is raised about understanding our communication across cultures. What may seem a simple, inoffensive statement in one language and culture may have a distinctly different meaning in another. How do you overcome this?

More than anything, these stories speak of the dreams, self - realisation, perseverance and fulfilment in each of the authors. Whether overcoming an abusive relationship, starting a new endeavour from scratch or discovering a new facet of themselves by living through a trauma or event that provides that "Aha" moment, each of these stories is worthy of your attention.

They are a good and timely reminder that not everyone is accorded the same opportunities and happiness as maybe you are. It's okay to question, doubt and then question some more if that is what it takes to fulfil the dreams you have for yourself. Most of all, heed the instruction to put your oxygen mask on first before assisting others to be of the most value to those around you!

Singapore Children's Society

Children's
SOCIETY
Caring for the Future

Founded in 1952, the mission of Singapore Children's Society is to bring relief and happiness to children in need. The Society protects and nurtures children and youth of all races and religions.

Singapore Children's Society currently operates more than10 service centres, offering services in the four categories of: Vulnerable Children and Youth, Children and Youth Services, Family Services, and Research and Advocacy.

Royalties through the sale of this volume will support the work of the Society which includes being a voice for our children and their future.

We are grateful for the trust that the authors and publishers of this book have shown in supporting our work. Without their collective voices this book would not exist.

For further information and to support the Society, visit our website at https://www.childrensociety.org.sg/

STORY ONE

Another Path, Another Way Forward

We all deserve to lead healthy, better, fulfilling, and easeful lives.

"I can't speak. I'm tired," the little boy whispers. "I understand," I whisper back. His mother speaks for him, despair etched on her weary face. "He was coughing again last night and crying all morning. He can't go to his friend's party today. He feels so left out."

With a personalised treatment plan that will allow her boy to break free from the shackles of asthma, mother and child leave the clinic.

But her words linger. *Left out.*

I'm transported back to the time when I was the wheezing kid. A three-year-old too young to fully comprehend my diagnosis nor the immense impact asthma would have on my life journey. I, too, felt left out when I missed weeks of nursery school. When school friends went to overnight camp, I stayed home, struggling to breathe. When as a runner and dancer, I pushed hard but didn't have the stamina to keep up with my peers.

At the same time, my childhood allowed me to experience life and learn differently – ways that have shaped the person I am today. Sprawled on the floor of our home study, the days passed quickly as I flipped through the pages of encyclopaedias, mesmerised by the human body's capabilities. On weekends, I listened eagerly as my grandmother – a worldly woman who loved and lived freely – told stories of her late father, a doctor and renowned diagnostician whose spiritual guidance I feel even today. And, as a white Jewish girl born and raised in South Africa, I witnessed the hatred of apartheid, all while my beloved nanny and a woman of colour tenderly cared for me on my sickest days.

From my earliest memories, I wanted to be a doctor – to heal and restore quality of life. I wanted to make the world a better place – to ensure everyone had a better way of being.

With dogged determination, I studied diligently to pursue my dreams and was ecstatic when I began my pre-med degree at Dartmouth College, USA. Little did I know sickness would derail my best-laid plans.

Just a few months in, projectile vomiting became my perplexing norm. Sitting in a study group for no reason that I could fathom at the time, I'd throw up violently. While training for track during spring break in Florida, I stress-fractured my spine – a consequence of osteopenia brought about by the steroid inhaler I'd been on since I was three. Anxiety ensued, and I suffered multiple panic attacks, not helped by the fact that I was trapped in a toxic relationship and living with an unstable roommate in a damp room.

At the student centre, I was prescribed anti-anxiety medication to be taken any time anxiety reared its ugly head. But with the medication, my semi-photographic memory began to falter. Retaining information became impossible; mentally, I had to push harder. By the third semester, extreme exhaustion crept in and, much to my chagrin, I could no longer cope. Drained and disheartened, I had to go home.

Returning for my second year, I knew slow and steady was the only way forward. But barely a month in, my symptoms resurfaced, and I was forced to take a leave of absence. Back in Cape Town, an infectious diseases doctor delivered a crushing blow. I had chronic fatigue syndrome – a debilitating disease that many conventional doctors misunderstand even today. “There’s nothing that can be done for you,” he advised.

He was wrong.

After a semester at the University of Cape Town, I returned to Dartmouth College. On medication and with provisions in place to pace myself, I was back on the path to my dream profession.

But the Universe had a different path for me.

During my summer break, while interning with Dr Barbara Silbert, a naturopathic doctor in Boston, I discovered the infinite potential of natural healing. At the end of my internship, this wonderful doctor, who I am still in touch with today, prescribed a homeopathic remedy that opened something deep inside me and shifted my perspective.

When I returned to university for my final year, and the symptoms hit hard, I understood what I needed to do. Trusting in the Universe, I withdrew from the university and ended my relationship. It was time to take the road less travelled.

Another path, another way forward.

Back home, while working at a pharmacy, I came across a book by acclaimed Canadian naturopath Michael Murray. With every page turned, I knew with greater clarity and conviction that this was the right path for me.

At the same time, my health trajectory was changing too. A quirky medical doctor prescribed Vitamin B12 shots and old-school antibiotics to treat the illness in my body, and I began to feel better.

But given the trauma I'd experienced, it was only a matter of time before a trigger would set my symptoms off. My mother turned to a practitioner friend for help. She healed me through holographic repatterning, empowering me to overcome past hurts and move forward to achieve my higher-level goals. That, combined with homeopathy, had the most incredible effect. Going from strength to strength, I was able to rebuild my life.

I completed a degree in nutrition at Kings College London, UK, and took up running and dancing again. I went to Southwest College of Naturopathic Medicine and Health Sciences, USA, to do a four-year doctorate in Naturopathic Medicine. I knew I was home from the first moment I stepped onto the college campus. When I trained under experts in homeopathy like Stephen Messer, I realised I was on a transformational journey.

I no longer felt left out. The world of naturopathy is where I belong.

True naturopathic medicine is the most beautiful system of medicine. It blends traditional therapeutic practices with modern medicine and today's science, offering the best of both worlds. As a naturopathic physician, I would have the skills to see beyond superficial symptoms and find every underlying factor within their being causing illness - the physical, mental, emotional, spiritual, and more. I could piece together the puzzle and create a holistic plan for long-term healing by combining ancient wisdom with modern science. Just the idea of what I could do for people filled me with passion and purpose.

It was a naturopathic doctor who kick-started my healing from asthma, naturally. She treated my gut with herbs, homeopathy, and lifestyle recommendations such as going gluten and dairy-free. She improved my mental well-being with colour puncture, and, with her help, I ditched a couple of my long-term medications.

Now thriving, I excelled in all my subjects. With improved energy, I took up tutoring, joined the student government, and took extra courses at the weekend.

But I was still dependent on my asthma inhaler and spray. After completing my doctorate and graduating top of my class, I stayed on for a one-year residency. Here, I met Dr Nathalie Ham, a second-year homeopathic resident, who completely transformed my health and helped me become medicine-free. To this day, Natalie remains my trusted homeopathic doctor.

During my residency year, I returned briefly to Cape Town for my father's 60th birthday and fell head over heels in love with my childhood friend. After completing my residency, I went back to be with him so that we could begin a life together.

I took a teaching job at the University of the Western Cape and later joined a private health practice. But I knew South Africa wasn't the right place for us. With my father living in Hong Kong and willing to help us, we moved there in May 2011.

In 2012, while working for other health and medical clinics, I attended a conference where I met the Founder and the Managing Director of Hong Kong's largest and leading natural health clinic, IMI – Integrated Medicine Institute. They asked me to join the clinic, and in 2014 I became a Partner and Director. Two years later, when they moved to the UK, I took on the role of Managing Director too. While maintaining my busy practice, I continue leading over 30 of the industry's finest practitioners and 20 staff to deliver a consistent wellness experience to more than 38,000 clients.

I have treated thousands of clients – from newborns to people in their 90s – with all kinds of acute and chronic health conditions. Children with allergies, asthma, and eczema; women with hormonal issues and autoimmune diseases; teens and adults with anxiety, depression, and work-life stress; couples with infertility and more.

I'm currently supporting my youngest son too who is on the autism spectrum. Taking an integrated approach to his health and well-being, I've been able to put the pieces of his health puzzle together to create a personalised healing plan, so my wonderful boy can thrive. Homeopathy, supplements, dietary tweaks, speech therapy, occupational therapy, and special needs support at school. He may be different, but – with the right kind of treatment – he does not have to feel left out. Recently, I received a call from the head of the Special Needs Department: she wanted to know how my son was doing so well and what could be done to help other children in her care do well too.

We all deserve to lead healthy, better, fulfilling, and easeful lives. That sad little boy breathing noisily in my treatment room shouldn't be held back by asthma. Nor should the baby howling with colic, the man defeated by burnout, or the woman distressed by fibromyalgia. I'm not just here to heal; I'm here to advocate for each person and their health.

Like many, you or a loved one may have been told that nothing can be done to heal you. You must live with your health condition, endure pain and discomfort, and base every decision you make on what can't be done because of your illness. You may have been told to pop pills to manage your condition or suppress your symptoms – sometimes they're needed when the body's organs are at a point when they can't be revived, but most times they're not.

With the right therapeutic conditions, your body has innate capabilities to heal itself. It won't be an overnight fix – doctors quick to prescribe pills and give band-aid solutions aren't looking to find and treat the root causes of your condition. It will take time and commitment to achieve long-term results. But one day, you, too, can be free from unnecessary medication, avoidable surgical procedures, and the cumbersome constraints that come with chronic health conditions.

Thirteen years on, I'm still medicine-free and leading a rich and rewarding life. Homeopathy, herbs, and supplements – all nature's wonders – allow me to be healthy and strong. Mentally and emotionally, homeopathy helps to keep my Type A personality in check – easing my worries and helping me cope with curveballs. On a physical level, just a few years ago, a bone density scan revealed my spine had completely healed from osteopenia. If I continued with the medications I was on; I would have osteoporosis.

I encourage you to advocate for yourself. Empower yourself on your journey to optimal health and well-being. You don't have to accept the rhetoric given to you. You don't have to continue along a path that is not truly serving you. There is always another path, another way forward.

ABOUT THE AUTHOR

DR. BENITA PERCH

Dr. Benita Perch is a multi-award-winning US-trained and licensed Naturopathic Physician, Homeopath, and Corporate Wellness Speaker with over a decade of experience treating acute and chronic diseases in thousands of infants, children, and adults across the globe.

She is the Managing Director of IMI – Integrated Medicine Institute, Hong Kong and Asia's largest and leading natural medicine clinic.

Taking a truly integrated approach to healing. Benita combines significant expertise in conventional pathology, modern diagnostic testing, functional medicine, pharmacology, homeopathy, herbal medicine, and clinical nutrition to treat the root causes of health issues for long-term healing.

Benita currently resides in Thailand with her husband and two sons.

You can connect with Dr. Benita at:

✉ : drbenitaperch@gmail.com

in : https://www.linkedin.com/in/benita-perch-nd/

STORY TWO

Believing in Myself and My Abilities

Serving as a powerful female role model for my daughter and other girls.

You are the architect of your own destiny; you are the master of your own fate; you are behind the steering wheel of your life. There are no limitations to what you can do, have, or be. Except the imitations you place on yourself by your own thinking.

— Brian Tracy

My Beginnings

When I reflect upon my earliest memories of my journey, I never predicted life would take me to extraordinary heights as an international businesswoman/CEO.

Growing up in Mumbai, I imagined a simple future for my life with few options. Almost any individual might feel somewhat insignificant in the pounding heart of India's cultural capital. So many people in one place, from the filthy rich to the dirt poor, with countless dreams immersed in rich, vivid colours and vibrant spiritual energy shining through every living thing. The streets were flooded with music and dance, and powerful aromas and flavours were found around every corner. Every person was doing business and whatever else they could to survive another day or make their fortunes in corporations and, most of all, the booming Bollywood film industry. During my childhood, I felt lost at the centre of the infinite Universe when I felt like a side character in my own movie, with no idea what I would do with my life or even what I could do with my life.

In contrast to my siblings, I was an ordinary student with

average grades during my boring years in grade school. My parents were often concerned about my future and how I would survive as a young woman in the harsh and competitive world. Any caring parent worries about how well their offspring will do when they finally leave the nest. This is especially true when those offspring fail to march in step with society along the guaranteed path to success and instead take the rocky road less travelled or wait until after school to spread wings and take flight into the bright unknown.

My family's concerns about me lessened after I got married. However, I felt stifled and restless in India, confined by ancient tradition in what I could accomplish. After facing challenges of self-doubt through preconceived notions of women and strict religion, I overcame these doubts.

Moving to Hong Kong with my husband, I was delighted to enter a new world of opportunities. An abundance of stimulating employment welcomed me to secure a real place of purpose within the tech industry. Stepping into the consultancy and recruitment world led me to transcend the qualities I felt I lacked and experience a world where my qualities are wanted, and my strengths are respected. Through this new environment in Hong Kong, I gained true independence.

One skill I learned around that time was to believe in myself and my abilities. Never again would I let the world, another person or even my insecurities lock me in a box of simple definitions. I realised I had a passionate strength and would be doing a disservice to myself and others if I let my innovative vision be clouded. It would be a shame to allow my driving force to better the world to be stopped by my preconceptions of other people's opinions about me. Ultimately, those limitations don't matter as much as what we do despite our personal obstacles.

It became clear that I should listen to my instinct and higher self and take responsibility for realising my dreams through direct action. Also, while it's important to dream big and believe in our inner power, it's important not to get so carried away by our passionate ideologies that we become unrealistic about our situation. Lastly, I would also say it's essential not to be too trusting of those who haven't earned our trust since not everyone has our best interests at heart.

My Achievements

"If you have the courage to start,
you have the courage to succeed".

— Mel Robbins

Becoming a mother was something I knew was part of my destiny. Following my daughter's birth, I learned so much about responsibility and devotion and how that new pure kind of mother-daughter love would push me to go beyond what was ever expected. A fire of duty ignited inside me, a desire to achieve something great beyond my wildest imagination and help create a better world for her.

By overcoming obstacles to start a business enterprise, I'd contribute to the world of opportunities for others, serving as a powerful female role model for her and other girls.

Determined after I decided to raise a business from the ground up, I partnered with an ex-colleague and started Career Works, an IT consulting and recruiting firm. After becoming the sole CEO and President of Career Works, I witnessed exponential market success and rapid growth across Hong Kong, resulting from my leadership and the contributions of my skilled staff members.

These days, Career Works is as active and progressive as ever, constantly evolving and expanding our influential presence in the global market. We now have a second office in Singapore, with ongoing expansion throughout Australia and my native India.

I'll never know whether I've been lucky or blessed. Still, I get empowered by seeing the continuous growth happening within and around me across these productive years as an entrepreneur. I feel proud knowing the future is brighter for women in business than it's maybe ever been. When we form effective support systems in the working world, we can better ensure the world continues to become equal and fair for everyone.

I am here to be a giver, giving most of my time and energy to the sustainable progress of those I work with, from my staff of five to the fifty to sixty contractors finding gainful employment through my cultivated business network, satisfied clients and business partners. Working to create guaranteed career opportunities for IT professionals on the global stage, I adapt to the constant changes in the world and the workforce.

For four years, I also served as the president of one of the major Indian Associations in Hong Kong, aiming to empower new and old transplants from my homeland, creating a solid support network and the Indian expat community.

Over life's ups and downs, via countless lessons learned and valuable knowledge gained, I've learned to remain careful and thoughtful regarding every decision I make and to not react too emotionally or negatively to unexpected curveballs.

The more I experience, the less bothered or insecure I feel about unforeseen things and the more comfortable I feel with my place in life. The fear I used to have growing up still lingers within me on some days. However, I can always breathe and remember how far I've come and what I've accomplished.

Reflecting on that reality, I liberate my mindset from that familiar old feeling of not being good enough compared to some impossible standard of perfection and our distorted perspective of others, who are also likely experiencing some type of doubt and insecurity.

The Learnings

"Let your actions be louder than your words and your dreams bigger than your fears."

— Invajy

Every person carries power and the potential to do something great. Discovering that power within myself has inspired one of the most rewarding transformations I could have asked for on my journey and a miracle I hope to help others find within where we often least expected it. It's a favour I can only hope to pay forward after having positive inspirations early in my career, such as my lifelong friends, who always believed in me and motivated me to be confident, resilient and ultimately a personal success.

Any person reading this can aspire to greatness they never imagined possible. An extraordinary life could be waiting around the corner if we work hard towards making our dreams into reality and never give up. You'll never know how life will turn out in your favour if you stay positive and devote yourself faithfully to your cause.

Before losing my parents in recent years, I could show them the life of success I created for myself despite the odds stacked against me. After so many years of their doting worries that I wouldn't make it in the adult world, seeing the pure pride in their shining eyes filled my heart with indescribable joy. This was the ultimate affirmation that my constant effort and innovative risks were worth it.

My advice for future generations, especially women looking to leave the ordinary existence behind to build an extraordinary legacy in this male-dominated global market, is this: Always remember the true importance of hard work, perseverance and patience along the chaotic twists and turns and ups and downs you are guaranteed to face on your journey toward greatness.

Here on earth, I remain devoted as a giver, working to help as many people as possible realise their dreams. Whether helping people discover a life-changing career path they love, assisting in attaining business or serving as president of a reputed association, I love serving others as a leader, however possible.

Even after many milestones and achievements thus far as a businesswoman, my journey is far from done. No retirement plans are in my near future, and neither is falling into patterns of complacency.

A burning curiosity for life and an insatiable hunger for knowledge continue to drive me daily. Life is like a classroom, and I love the idea of constantly gaining new knowledge and wisdom until the end of this life and possibly the next life.

As a devout Hindu, my universal faith in God has only become stronger, as I believe accumulating the best karma and helping the most people in this life is one of the most honourable goals. What we do and the legacy we leave behind matters.

These days I only feel more passionate about life. I look forward to a brighter future and more precious time spent studying more fields of expertise. Striving to continue becoming a better person than I was yesterday, I will keep working to stimulate growth and opportunity for others every day and keep cherishing and giving back to the people I love most. I hope to share the story of my conscious evolution from an ordinary life as a young girl to an extraordinary existence as a successful woman to encourage others to do the same!

ABOUT THE AUTHOR

BIJAL JHAVERI

Bijal Jhaveri is the founder and CEO of The Career Works. She has offices in Hong Kong, Singapore and India.

A shy, submissive, and docile girl who only did what she was told and was often overpowered by her intelligent siblings has broken all the barriers and mastered her destiny and faith. Her to-do attitude, positivity, resilience, and trust in God have helped her reach her destiny. She has immense belief in making things happen.

She is a mother of one daughter and is blessed with loads of love and blessings from family and friends.

She believes if you trust yourself, have the courage and trust your decisions; you can achieve your wildest dreams.

Her goal in life is not to give up, to work hard, help others and keep upgrading her skills by studying.

You can connect with Bijal at:

✉ : bijal@thecareerworks.com

in : https://www.linkedin.com/in/bijal-jhaveri-2635111/

STORY THREE

Finding Joy and Purpose Outside my Comfort Zone

And I did.

"I've been offered an incredible job opportunity – in Amsterdam," I said to my husband in December 2017. We had been married since 1998 and built a comfortable life together at our home in Ontario, Canada. My husband had worked tirelessly over the years, building his own business while I completed my education and established my career.

I enjoyed volunteering on several boards of directors with not-for-profit organisations. I worked near Toronto and led a small team of three regulatory professionals. I was a member of the local management team. I was well-respected internally and externally; my personal leadership brand was known and valued. I was thriving in my comfort zone. The company I worked for was in the process of a massive restructuring, dividing into two business units.

Big changes were coming. Fortunately, three senior leaders sponsored me for a stretch role in the new organisation. After much deliberation, careful consideration, and a massive leap into the unknown, we agreed that such an opportunity doesn't happen that often, and I would try it for a year.

Due to the nature of his business, my husband would need to remain in Canada, and I would head to Amsterdam alone. I am forever grateful for his enduring support and belief.

The next few months were a blur, as I prepared for this adventure – with equal amounts of fear and anticipation. I had never lived or worked outside of Canada. On March 1, 2018, I landed in Amsterdam with two heavy suitcases, some self-doubt, and a very heavy heart after leaving my loved ones back at home. However, I did not permit wasted energy to be spent on feeling sad or sorry for myself – I had too much to prove to those who had believed in me. I felt a big obligation not to disappoint those who had advocated, encouraged, and supported me.

I immersed myself in the new job while learning how to navigate living abroad independently. The Netherlands is an easy place to be a native English speaker. I developed an affection for a country that afforded a safe and welcoming environment for ex-pats. I took Dutch language lessons and soon found I wouldn't have much opportunity to practice. When I would try to speak Dutch, the locals would immediately answer me in English. Oh well, I tried!

At work, I was outside my comfort zone in my new role as the Global VP Regulatory for one of the new business units. I had end-to-end responsibility in 70+ countries, 15 senior leaders as direct reports and a global team of 170 employees. I worked with the most senior people in the organisation, many of whom operated in a different style than my own. The norm was an outdated command-and-control, macho style of leadership. Many times I was the only woman in the boardroom.

I'm naturally introverted, deep thinker needing more time to process information before moving to a decision. My preference is to listen more than I speak. This doesn't come at the expense of delivery or achievement – I can also be very impatient (I now reframe this as having a bias for action) and very self-critical. Imposter syndrome doesn't even begin to describe how I felt most of the time, and it didn't feel good.

The expectations, responsibility and stakes were high, and I knew I had to quickly establish and prove my credibility, competence, and value. However, I convinced myself that to accomplish these things, I couldn't show up fully as myself. There wasn't enough time to cultivate and establish my own authentic brand. The hours were long and intense. I told myself I needed to conform to the "heroic leader knows all" style I was surrounded by.

That was one of many lessons that year.

It wasn't always a struggle. I met some incredible people through work, many of who had also recently relocated to the Netherlands. In many ways, it was a shared experience, and we formed deep, lasting bonds. It's a real gift to work for a global organisation with colleagues from all over the world, which opened my eyes and perspectives. In those social moments when I was "just me," it felt so freeing and comfortable, yet I still held back most of the time when I was in work mode. At work, it was exciting to build something new together and start to make our mark in the organisation.

My team started to come together and find common ground. I realised that the command and control, the leader-knows-all approach was ineffective and not sustainable. While uncomfortable, I realised I needed to pivot to lead through others rather than be the "doer" myself.

This required a lot of trust between myself and my leadership team – a test of my vulnerability and resilience. It wasn't comfortable or easy. Playing a role that wasn't fully me was exhausting – in fact, I recently heard it expressed in this way: "there is a reason why professional theatre actors sleep a lot during the day – it's because they play someone else each night and it's very tiring to do that for long periods of time." I fully agree!

Looking back, I didn't see how close I was to burning out and losing myself entirely in the process. Being separated for weeks, sometimes months, from my husband and family was way harder than I could have imagined, plus the demands of the job were incessant. I wasn't prioritising my needs – to recharge my battery, connect with my loved ones, volunteer, or take the time for rest. Yet, despite this, I was impacting my team, peers, and stakeholders. The role I was playing was paying off in terms of delivery, reputation, and presence, but at great personal expense. At this pace, I was on a path to failing one way or another.

It was mine to lose. Until I had a lightbulb moment.

Near the end of the year, I participated in an externally facilitated workshop with cross-functional colleagues on Impactful Presence & Presentation Skills. The coaches were incredibly supportive and pushed us out of our comfort zone. After all, that's where all the best learning and growth come from, right?

As the program neared the end, they gave us a challenging assignment. We were given five minutes to prepare a five-minute talk describing a difficult moment in our lives and what we learned from it. We then took turns delivering the talk to the group while the facilitators made observations. There was something beautiful and safe in the atmosphere they had created, and I decided to deliver that talk as my true self at that moment.

And I did.

The talk flowed naturally, and while it was describing a difficult moment, I felt pretty good about it even though my inner self-critic thought it could have been better. The facilitator began her feedback with a question. She said, "Do you know how amazing you are?" At that moment, the cumulative effects of that year came to a crescendo, and her feedback deeply moved me. I cried. And I realised she was a mirror reflecting what she saw in my true self. At that moment, she challenged me to accept that I am enough just as I am—more than enough.

From then on, I was more mindful of quieting my inner critic, operating more authentically and naturally and prioritising my own time for activities that bring me joy and recharge, including being with my loved ones, volunteering, and learning.

It didn't happen overnight, and some days are better than others. The differences were subtle, although I was sitting in the boardroom with the business unit president a few months later. We were chit-chatting until the rest of the team arrived. He looked at me with a boyish grin and said, "You aren't the typical Reckitt leader", to which I replied with an equally big grin and said, "I know, and that is what makes me awesome."

He laughed and nodded in agreement. Progress had been made, and, at that moment, my inner self-critic was silenced.

I continued to work with those coaches on my leadership journey, refining my purpose and building skills to maximise my impact in an authentic style. In 2019, this team of coaches designed and delivered a multi-year program on inclusive and expansive leadership with my leadership team.

This commitment to our individual and collective learning continued through the pandemic and is a key factor in our success. We have built a solid foundation of trust, candid dialogue, accountability, safety, and deep care. This also took time and effort and still does today. Our team's why and purpose is tangible to those we lead and our peers. It's described as a "type of magic" by colleagues. We aim to show the way for others and share what we have learned along the way. It's one of my proudest achievements in this role.

I was so inspired by the impact made by those coaches that I began a program of study in 2020 to obtain my own Organizational and Relationship Systems Coaching education through Schouten University in the Netherlands. I've been a life-long learner with insatiable curiosity. The two-year program of study was challenging. I learned a lot about myself. I'm so grateful for the meaningful connections made with more coaches helping make the world kinder and gentler.

Systems Inspired Leadership is a powerful alternative for leading in a VUCA (volatile, uncertain, complex and ambiguous) world. In contrast to the command and control, a leader-knows-all approach, which leads to pressure, stress and burnout, systems-inspired leaders leverage the collective wisdom and power of the team. It creates a robust, collaborative "we" culture, enhanced agility, skilful change navigation and engaged employees.

These days, I intentionally demonstrate my unique style of leadership. I don't pretend to be someone else. We need positive portrayal to help others believe there is no one-size-fits-all type of leader. It requires much less energy to be your authentic self. I mentor and informally coach and value the learning I receive from my mentees and colleagues. I volunteer within and outside the organisation on topics I care about. I continue to work with those same coaches who gave me my lightbulb moment. I read and learn actively from my network. I prioritise trips home to spend with those I love. These activities bring me joy since they link directly to my personal why to unleash the potential in others and bring more humanity to work.

As I reflect on how far I have come since that conversation in 2017, I'd like to offer three pieces of advice to my former self. I hope you will find them helpful.

> Deeply self-reflect. Are you showing up as your authentic self in all aspects of your life? If not, pinpoint where you are "playing a role" and observe the impact on your physical and mental well-being. Take small actions to shed the act and note the difference.
>
> Quiet your inner critic and learn to be your own champion. I often say I give great advice to others and

am not great at following it myself. Follow your own advice! You are wise with a lot to offer, don't hold back. Surround yourself with people who can be the mirror you need, especially when you have self-doubt.

One of my favourite quotes is, "A curious mind knows no limits – Anonymous." Never stop learning and prioritising your own personal development needs. Lean into where you may be uncomfortable – that's where all the growth happens, and it's immensely rewarding. You will become a better human.

ABOUT THE AUTHOR

HEATHER BARKER

Heather Barker is the Global VP of Regulatory at consumer goods company Reckitt in Amsterdam. She is also the VP, Board of Directors for A.I.S.E. (International Association for Soaps & Detergents). In 2020 she was selected for one of ten industry seats on the EU Commission High-Level Roundtable for the Chemicals Strategy for Sustainability.

A curious systems-inspired leader, Heather is the Executive sponsor for the LGTBQ+ ERG as an ally, a member of the Inclusion Board at Reckitt and volunteers with the Netherlands chapter of LEAD (Leading Executives Advancing Diversity).

She is often invited as an industry speaker, coach and mentor. She finds joy in helping others fully realise their potential as their authentic selves. "Be a better human" is her motto.

Heather has a BSc in Biochemistry (Minor in Nutritional Science) and an MSc in Toxicology. She also holds an Organizational & Relationship Systems Coaching (ORSC™) certification from Schouten University.

You can connect with Heather at:

✉ : heatherjbarker@gmail.com

in : https://www.linkedin.com/in/heather-barker-she-her-2813416/

f : https://www.facebook.com/hjbarker

STORY FOUR

Getting Comfortable being in Uncomfortable Situations

There is nothing wrong with being comfortable in your comfort zone.

How often have you heard or seen the phrase "stepping out of your comfort zone"? Do a quick Google image search for "comfort zone", and you will see multiple diagrams showing and explaining the different zones you will be stepping into when you step out of your comfort zone.

I'll be honest – I love such diagrams and structures, and I would be lying if I said that I have not unequivocally placed myself in the zone with which I resonated the most (hint: it is not the comfort zone). But am I supposed to feel uncomfortable if I am not in my comfort zone? Why, then, do I still feel comfortable enough to exist in an ever-changing environment?

Perhaps the simple actions I have learnt and chosen to take over the years bring a sense of familiarity and safety to me, even as the routines in my personal and professional life and my social interactions continue to shift.

After all, what's wrong with being comfortable in the comfort zone anyway?

Stay with what you do know – Listen and Learn

Everyone speaks about networking these days – whether for work, professional opportunities or even in social settings to widen your social circle. Unless you live under a rock, it is entirely possible that you may have been asked to present at work, attend an industry-specific conference or join a social networking lunch or dinner. Of course, the whole idea of doing so is to create exposure, network and connect, and not just be in attendance speaking amongst people you already know.

I used to be from what we call the sell-side of business in the financial services industry as an external auditor. And being a senior audit manager, business development became one of my key performance indicators when my bosses assessed my annual work. This meant having to attend industry-wide conferences to network and introduce myself to potential clients, understand what they do, and quickly gauge what types of services our company could offer as a solution.

In case you are wondering, I am an accountant by training and not in sales or marketing for a reason, so for an introvert like myself, going up to business professionals to inject myself into conversations and weave in a sales pitch drove my anxiety level up. I never got the hang of it back then, and my attendance at such events honestly did not gain my company many new clients.

Looking back, however, what did contribute to my business development performance indicator was when I created additional revenue streams from my existing audit clientele. I achieved this by understanding and anticipating my clients' changing needs and providing add-on services such as annual trainings for their in-house accounting teams on new accounting standards, customised to new accounting standards that would impact my clients.

Whenever new tax regulations were announced, I proactively connected my clients to my tax advisory colleagues for consultancy solutions on how such new tax regulations impacted them.

So stay with what you do know – in this case, I already had a working rapport with my existing audit clientele, so selling to them was significantly less daunting. I found my comfort zone by listening and learning from them about what they were planning for the future, then taking time to find a solution instead of doing a sales pitch on the fly.

It helps always to ask the right questions, which encourages listening and learning.

Find your allies - Fake it till you make it (without arrogance)

Fast forward a few years, and I still had not overcome how uncomfortable I felt being alone in a room full of strangers. I plead momentary insanity when I had agreed to attend an acquaintance's fund-raising event for a cause I honestly do not now recall. Perhaps it was the feeling that it was for a charitable cause, so I felt obliged to attend the event even though I did not know anyone there other than my acquaintance. I also did not think of bringing a plus-one since not everyone may feel the same about charitable fund-raising events.

I only spoke with the acquaintance for a brief minute that entire evening. I was left standing by myself, occasionally helping myself to the buffet and eating in awkward silence amidst a room filled with people chatting and laughing. While I was feeling embarrassed for myself, a lady approached me to start a conversation and introduced herself as Eva. She had also attended the event solo and asked me a few questions to make small talk. She seemed rather genuine, and just as I was warming up to her, she said, "Well, it was lovely to meet you, Angela. Maybe I will see you around later." She then smiled and walked away.

Not knowing what to do with myself right after, I stood rooted in place and noticed Eva had walked off to approach another person who appeared to be attending the event solo. From my observation, they did not appear to know each other before the event.

I am not a stalker by any means, but I did notice that Eva did the same thing to walk away a few minutes later and went on repeat to approach another person standing alone by the buffet. I imagined she probably asked the same few questions of each person for small talk and then moved on again.

Of course, I found it insincere and borderline arrogant to interact in a social setting like how Eva did. On reflection, however, I realised she was opportunistic in seeking out other solo attendees like myself as her allies to interact with instead of standing awkwardly alone the whole time.

I do this from time to time now – fake confidence at social gatherings or professional events by approaching people who look like they would welcome company, to be my allies. After the initial exchange of names, I would ask them questions like "How do you know the host?" and "What do you do for a living?" Unlike Eva, though, I try to stay with the small talk, listening, learning, and asking more questions instead of walking away too quickly as if on repeat. While faking confidence does get easier with practice, I find it helps to remain sincere while faking it till you make it.

I do the same when I must make a big presentation at work. I will find allies amongst my colleagues before the actual presentation to do a dry run rehearsal with and have them ask me questions as if they were participants in the actual presentation. This gets me in a more comfortable position ahead of presentation day, and less faking of confidence is required. It helps if these allies are actual participants on the day of the presentation itself.

As an introvert, I will never be 100% comfortable doing so, and there will be hits and misses. I have made a few real friends and allies through such interactions, but I have also been "walked away from" (again) many times. Well, that's when I go on repeat at the next opportunity.

Control your emotions

Change sometimes throws us a curveball and makes for uncomfortable situations in life. It is only human to feel a range of emotions when a curveball strikes you unexpectedly. Some time ago, a friend of mine – let's call her Sara – joined a new company as it was getting too busy for her at her previous employer. It was a gamble she was willing to take, given that she was in her forties and the new company was growing. For context, most recruiters in Singapore would view jobseekers over forty as being old for the mid-level role that Sara was at.

Given that her new company was small, Sara felt her years of experience would allow her to shine and showcase herself to her bosses. A few months into her new role, Sara came to a group of us as friends to vent her frustrations that the expectations at her new company were too high and unreasonable, given the size.

On top of that, she was not accorded the same autonomy and respect that she was used to at her previous company. We supported her as friends to hang in there and find her place as she was still settling into the role.

Within six months, Sara's discomfort escalated to a level that caused some alarm to us as her friends. She shared more instances of unhappiness in her job and started blaming her colleagues and bosses for the situation. There were many sessions where tears were shed, and we were concerned for Sara's mental and emotional well-being. Eventually, Sara threw in the towel within a year, and while it took her some time to find another role, it was probably the right decision.

Whether it is higher demands at the workplace or home, a change of environment, having to take (or give) critical feedback or bad news, or simply having differences in opinions with the people around us, it is easy to lose control of our emotions and let our egos, fear, self-doubt, anxiety, and stress get the better of us. As observers and friends, we saw flashes of defensiveness, anger, negativity, and passive-aggressiveness present themselves in Sara's description of events.

When placed in uncomfortable situations, it is important to find an outlet for our emotions – some find this in exercising, meditation, enjoying a cup of coffee or spending time with loved ones. It is even more important to learn to accept the uncomfortable situations we are in sometimes and control our emotions before they overwhelm us. Easier said than done, but to get comfortable being in uncomfortable situations, we sometimes just need to be kind to ourselves and to others around us. There are no winners in holding onto self-destructive emotions.

Expanding your comfort zone

Remember when I said there is nothing wrong with being comfortable in your comfort zone? Indeed, everything we do in life should make our lives easier and more comfortable. In fact, every great invention in history was created to bring us more convenience. I can only imagine why asking someone to "step out of their comfort zone" seems ridiculous. Why would you want to be uncomfortable?

But think of the contrary idea: no one steps out of their comfort zone, everything in our surroundings remains familiar, change and great inventions cease to exist, and we all feel safe and secure. Isn't this also a ridiculous notion?

So how about choosing to add to our life's toolkit the actions we can take to get ourselves comfortable when life brings about uncomfortable situations?

Stay with what you do know, Listen and Learn, Find your allies, Fake it till you make it (without arrogance) and Control your emotions – these actions aren't asking you to step out of your comfort zone. Once we choose to get comfortable in uncomfortable situations, our comfort zone just expands, and there is no stepping out to speak of.

We will merely be getting ourselves comfortable in our ever-expanding comfort zones – Who's with me?

ABOUT THE AUTHOR

ANGELA KAM

Angela Kam is an optimistic realist – passionate about collecting and sharing memories to connect and inspire. Having lived and worked in Asia, Europe and the Caribbean, Angela is energised in a multicultural environment and considers herself an empathetic listener. A CPA and MBA holder with a Graduate Diploma in Organisational Psychology, she is a seasoned finance professional in the investment and asset management industry by day.

Growing up in Singapore, her early exposure to acts of altruism and volunteering planted a seed in Angela to always be kind. When she is not conscientiously checking off items on her bucket list, Angela enjoys relaxing with her favourite cup of coffee while reading or catching up with family and friends to exchange stories and create more memories.

You can connect with Angela at:

✉ : helloitsme.ange@gmail.com

in : https://www.linkedin.com/in/angela-k-singapore/

STORY FIVE

Hope, Possibility, and Designing Collaborative Futures

When you engage the right people, with the right process, focused on the right problem - Anything is possible.

Have you ever experienced the dark feeling of overwhelm when faced with a complex problem? It doesn't have to be this way. Valuable things can emerge from challenging or terrible circumstances. Let me explain how.

Just over a decade ago, a life-altering event sparked my passion for collaborative design – the art of bringing people together for a purpose. I'll share a few things I've learnt, but first, I'd like to take you back in time.

It's February 22, 2011, in Christchurch, my hometown in New Zealand. I'm at work in Cathedral Square in the city, getting ready to head out for lunch when BANG! The floor underneath me starts shaking violently. I dive under my desk for safety.

While under my desk, I can hear shelves from around the office fall to the ground. The shaking is so violent that I'm holding onto the legs of the desk to stop myself from getting thrown around. One of my colleagues is still standing. She can see outside the window and cries, "The Cathedral has fallen! People will have died! People will have died!"

Five months earlier, we'd had a large earthquake in Christchurch. While it was significant enough to damage several buildings in the city because it happened at 4:30 am, most people were in the relative safety of their homes, and casualties were minimal. I close my eyes, take deep breaths, and hold on tighter, praying for the shaking happening now to stop.

I'm terrified that the floor underneath me might give way. I'm scared for my loved ones, wondering where they are right now, whether they're feeling this as well, and whether they're safe. I'm also feeling uncertain about what's going to happen at this moment, how long it'll last and whether I'll even walk out of this building.

I later found out that 185 people lost their lives in the most devastating earthquake the city had ever endured.

Once the shaking settled, my colleagues and I gathered outside the open space, checking everyone was okay. While aftershocks continued to rumble around us, we hugged and cried in disbelief at what was happening. We slowly and cautiously made our way out of the city on foot. I stepped over huge cracks in concrete roads, saw cars compressed like pancakes under fallen brick building facades and walked through dust and clouds of building debris.

My colleague and I walked to her apartment so she could drive me home. I'd driven to work that day, but I couldn't get to my car – it was sitting in a car park building, and it would be some weeks before I could access it again.

Arriving home, I noticed a huge pile of sandy mud was now in the driveway. There was also a light covering of this substance all up the street. This heavy sludge was called liquefication and had been shaken up to above street level during the earthquake. Liquefaction was hard to move and covered streets and suburbs and made its way deep into people's homes.

My colleague waited in her car outside. I was going to run inside, pack an overnight bag, and she would take me to a friend's house so I wouldn't be alone in the townhouse I rented while the aftershocks continued. Structurally, from the outside, the house looked sound. I cautiously tip-toed inside and was met with broken glassware, picture frames and books across the floor. Everything that was previously on a shelf was now on the ground. Resisting the urge to pick things up, I made my way up the stairs into my bedroom.

Usually a tidy person, it was jarring to see my room in such disrepair. Among other things, my tall boy dresser had fallen forward, splaying the contents of my drawers all over the carpet. I noticed this feeling and felt guilty reminding myself to have perspective – there was so much worse happening elsewhere.

Regaining focus, I packed a bag. It was then the emotion of the last few hours hit. I sobbed in a way I could only do alone and in my empty house full of broken things. I thought about what I'd pack if I never came back – just in case another huge earthquake rumbled us again. I packed sentimental jewellery, a hard drive of photos, my laptop and some clothes.

In the coming days, weeks, and months, I worked closely with my family, friends, and colleagues to literally pick up the pieces of our lives and our city. The skyline of Christchurch changed forever. Hundreds of thousands of buildings and a lot of the city's infrastructure were broken or damaged. The central city was cordoned off with large barricades manned by the army to prevent people from entering while it was still an unsafe area. I watched on the news as six hundred emergency workers arrived from all over the world to help search for survivors in a mammoth recovery effort.

However, I saw a beautiful thing happen through the city's grief, devastation, and pain. Groups of everyday people organised themselves into volunteer groups to help the city and those in need.

Eight hundred farmers from surrounding areas formed the Farmy Army, organising themselves with their large farm machinery and muscles. They came into the city to help clear debris. A whopping ten thousand university students formed the Student Volunteer Army. Unable to access the university buildings, this huge group armed themselves with shovels and gumboots and distributed themselves around the city's most devastated communities to help clear debris and liquefaction from homes and driveways. And more than three hundred and fifty home bakers made baked goods in their own kitchens, bringing food into the city to help feed and nurture the exhausted rescue workers.

Seeing this happen took me from a place of darkness to light. I felt proud. Proud to be part of the story of the rebuild. It also gave me hope. Not only for the recovery of the city and the communities in it, but seeing this first-hand gave me hope that we as humans can create positive change for ourselves and the common good, even in the hardest of circumstances.

It also ignited something in me that made me deeply curious. How were these people coming together to do something so coordinated and effective for the greater good in this emotive, ambiguous, and highly complex situation? It wasn't something I'd witnessed before on this scale, and its beauty and power felt extremely transformative. I wanted to learn more about it. Why did it happen? And is it possible to create more of this on a large and small scale?

So, armed with these two questions and a burning desire to help create a better future, I pivoted my career and discovered the field of Collaborative Design. In my discovery, I found this modern approach to work and problem-solving, and it's been my passion for the last ten years.

Described as both an art and a science, Collaborative Design is a methodology where trained facilitators bring groups of people together in a way that allows them to solve complex problems in accelerated timeframes. While Collaborative Design draws from many schools of thought, the primary one I learnt from was MG Taylor™. It works by applying principles of psychology, architecture, behavioural science, education, and human-centred design, to how people think, interact, and work together. What I learnt is that when you engage the right people, with the right process, in the right problem, anything is possible.

It disrupts the traditional approach to "work" and getting things done from a top-down, siloed approach to a more collaborative, knowledge-sharing way of working where everyone is aligned to one shared goal, and everyone holds part of a solution.

Over the last decade, I've worked with governments, not-for-profits and Fortune 100 companies, successfully using this methodology to help them solve their most complex challenges and tackle their biggest opportunities. I've regularly seen teams do 12 months of work together in two days and create outcomes that far superseded their expectations of what they thought they could achieve.

Those participating are invited to face ambiguity, sit in silence, listen to different viewpoints, and stress test and iterate solutions. Outcomes include a sense of responsibility, empowerment and ownership of decisions and actions as stakeholders are encouraged to bring their own individual value and contribution to the table, just like the volunteers did following the earthquake.

Looking to others to deliver all aspects of a solution doesn't have to be the only way. Whether it be a governing body or an established organisation, it's helpful to know additional possibilities and outcomes may be gained when others are called to action around a common problem.

If you have something in your life you need to solve and there's no clear answer, here are some simple things I've learnt from my study of Collaborative Design Methodology that might be helpful for you today:

Before you start anything, get clear about what you want to do. If you're working with others, this means getting on the same page about your objectives. If possible, being in the same room or at least the same phone or Zoom call helps to speed this up. Nailing the objectives might be an iterative process where you are continually refining the wording, and that's ok because being clear about what you want to achieve can be easier than it sounds. However, once you land and all agree on this – it provides a clear guidepost for your work and an anchor point to rally around.

Adopt a curious mindset. You need to think differently to come up with new ways of thinking. Actively explore different points of view and engage in deep listening. Be conscious of your own biases that may arise during this process, and do your best to park them.

People power. Once you have the scope of what you're doing, it's time to get people involved. Invite people to join who are invested in the outcome. Inviting a diverse group is also helpful as they will provide a broad range of ideas, experience, subject matter expertise, resources and relationships to help you achieve the objectives.

If you can't have fun with a problem, you're not going to solve it. Humans are naturally creative, innovative, and collaborative, but we're not often surrounded by the conditions or circumstances that allow us to be this way. Play creates flow, which opens up a world of creativity that helps us think in new ways. For more information on this, search online for "MG Taylor Axioms" and also "Csikszentmihalyi flow".

Clearly capturing outcomes. Ensure final decisions, including actions and owners, are documented. This might be a simple list of bullet points or, for a more extensive project, a detailed table showing interdependencies and key milestones. Either way, capture actions live in the presence of those participating to ensure alignment and ownership.

Living in an increasingly complex world that's in the midst of being transformed by another new wave of technology, climate change, and a global health crisis, there are so many possibilities for collaborative design and its ability to help solve complex problems of today and tomorrow.

From what I have lived and learnt, my message to you today is one of possibility and hope. Possibility – that when you're faced with a difficult challenge, either in your personal life, in business, or something bigger you might be seeing in the world, there are tools to help you solve them. And hope – that we can create a better future for ourselves.

ABOUT THE AUTHOR

EMILY PEARSON

Emily Pearson is passionate about awakening groups' and individuals' collective power and potential to solve complex problems and enable positive change.

In 2011 Emily's life changed forever after finding herself in the heart of Christchurch, New Zealand, during a destructive 6.3 magnitude earthquake.

Inspired by the innovation and ingenuity of the post-quake volunteer groups, Emily left behind her career as a Marketing Executive in pursuit of learning more about and engineering 'collaboration' with a desire to help make the world a better place.

For the past ten years, now based in Sydney, Emily has worked with hundreds of industry leaders applying best practice collaborative design methodologies, delivering collaborative workshops for government, not-for-profit organisations and Fortune 100 companies.

Emily's desire is to help lead positive change in the world. Through her studies in psychology, human consciousness, and collective intelligence, she believes humanity can create a better, more sustainable future.

You can connect with Emily at:

✉ : emilystravels@gmail.com

in : https://www.linkedin.com/in/emily-pearson-/

STORY SIX

Improving Health Outcomes for Women

Know your worth and be proud of your power, grit and resilience during challenging times.

This is a meandering tale of an incomplete quest, a puzzle still missing some pieces if you will.

Let me start here by asking how many of you feel that there is great injustice in this world. And how many of you would like to make a difference?

Imagine a world where children are immune to tropical diseases and absolutely free to live their dreams. Many people talk about compassion. However, only a few practice it. According to my spiritual leader, compassion is empathy plus courageous action.

I'd like to share a story about a little girl in Hong Kong.

Occasionally on Sundays, the whole family – mum, dad, and their two daughters, would go to the beach at Repulse Bay. Like most fun-loving children, they would swim and splash in the sea and build sandcastles.

Unfortunately, the little girl fell sick. She had frequent headaches, fever, and muscle pain which the doctors diagnosed as the common flu; this continued week after week with no new diagnosis. She became sicker and sicker. She ended up in a hospital Intensive Care Unit. It became a matter of life or death.

A specialist doctor in Hong Kong diagnosed the little girl with a deadly viral infection of the brain. One morning, she woke up and cried out, "Mummy! Why is it so dark? I can't see.

She had gone blind. She was petrified. She heard her mother sobbing and couldn't understand what was happening around her. It was a desperately sad and distressing scene.

Although the doctors had finally diagnosed the illness correctly, her treatment would take months. She was required to have strong cortisone injections and had to learn how to walk again.

Yet the ordeal was not over. To find out whether the treatment had worked, the doctors in Hong Kong suggested a CT scan of the brain. The little girl and her parents had to fly to Great Ormond Street Children's Hospital in London for the scan. Well, that little girl was me, and thankfully, I survived.

I was a lucky survivor because I received timely care and treatment. We were blessed to have had relatives in London who helped my parents arrange appointments with the children's hospital specialists. Many other children in Asia die because they are either too poor or live too remotely to receive adequate care. And even more sadly, because their parents are not educated and have access to basic medical care and advice.

Growing up, I was always passionate about biology and chemistry at school. I was particularly fascinated with living organisms and how the whole process of life worked. This passion drove me to complete my Doctorate successfully and do research on the biochemistry of tropical diseases. Because of my experience as a desperately ill child, I have immense empathy for children in Asia who are less fortunate, especially mothers and their children in my home country of Bangladesh.

My parents are immensely kind and generous people. They founded an orphanage in a village called Faridpur in rural Bangladesh. As a consequence of my experience as an incredibly unwell child, I have a passion and desire to help children who may not have the means for medical treatment. I want to set up a health clinic in the same village to diagnose and treat diseases correctly.

I was fortunate to be born into a family that had the means to support my ill health. This made me intensely aware that we all have our own experiences and unique life stories. Every day the world lays witness to terrible events and injustice. The poor, underprivileged, and undeserving are often the victims of these life-changing events.

At the end of December 2019, I moved from Singapore to Kuala Lumpur with my husband because of his corporate job. Then COVID-19 hit, and we were stuck in lockdown. This caused me to go through difficult emotions, like anger or anxiety.

Over the past couple of years, we have all faced challenges due to the COVID-19 pandemic. Unexpected events or shocks, like the impact of COVID-19, disrupted our everyday routines, jolted us out of our comfort zones, and led me to ask big questions about what matters and what is worth doing. That anger got funnelled, channelled and then finally transformed into positive energy that ultimately made me pivot my career interests from pure life sciences, to healthcare and then to Artificial Intelligence (AI) meets healthcare, a part of the growing Health-tech industry.

I decided to use the COVID-19 time to reskill. My survival approach has been to return, to throw myself into some challenging artificial intelligence and disruptive technologies programs from MIT, IBM, and Google. I have kept my promise and commitment to life-long learning and successfully gained further certifications in applying these technologies within the healthcare industry (my true passion). However, this process still needed to be improved because it did not boost my psychological and motivational levels. There was still something more to be done. I realised that I would have to do something new and different to be able to fulfil my quest of helping others less fortunate.

It's no wonder many people, including myself, are rethinking their careers during the current post-pandemic times. We have faced challenges related to losing loved ones in the family and challenges associated with restarting careers and life after a two-year hiatus. At a subconscious level, the energy that enabled me as a little girl to survive and drove me to complete my PhD in Biochemistry was spontaneously aroused within me a third time to review my life and pivot my career in an unfolding and emerging post-pandemic world.

But is this the right time? Even for those lucky enough not to be sick, caring for others who are suffering, or scrambling to make ends meet, the pandemic has increased uncertainty and caught us unprepared in all ways. The situation feels both threatening and scary. And, as psychologists have shown, dire situations prompt us to behave conservatively.

In the middle of the confusion that a career change can bring, many of us hope that introspection will eventually produce a flash of blinding insight. But as I learned in my solitary contemplation and concurrent research, when not coupled with active experimentation, it is dangerous because it can lead us to get stuck in the realm of daydreams — which, of course, provide neither gainful employment nor personal fulfilment.

Self-reflection is best nourished by engaging in conversations and social exchanges with kindred spirits who respond, sympathise, commiserate, question, read your body language, and share their own experiences. That means getting together with a diverse group of people and friends and talking over lunch, dinner, or yoga sessions.

In the end, when it comes to restarting your life and reinventing your career during this once-in-a-lifetime crisis, remember this vital point – the time to get going is now, but you don't have to go it alone.

I am human, and venturing into uncharted territory can be nerve-wracking. Whenever I feel discomfort, I think about what I can control and cannot. I can control my home environment, where I spend my time, what I choose to learn, and the skills I need to hone. I cannot control the external environment and other people.

My advice for making decisions that matter is to remember that nothing lasts forever. As you get more practised in navigating the unknown, that feeling of discomfort becomes an indicator that you are on the right track.

I am still on my journey of self-discovery, especially after this temporary global pandemic hiatus. What are the concrete steps necessary for the next phase of my journey?

Staying positive is step one, and step two is re-skilling and re-inventing myself to drive that step forward. Step three is active networking, and step four is to be proud of my power, grit, and resilience during challenging times.

I am still searching for my perfect place in the world. There is still a disconnect between what I have already accomplished and what is critical for landing that dream role – if that even exists.

During this search, I have been researching and reading about what's vital for women's health of a certain age and maturity. What are the products and services that focus primarily on women?

I have discovered the term "FemTech", first coined in 2016 by entrepreneur Ida Tin. FemTech has grown to encompass a range of technology-enabled, consumer-centric products and solutions in just a few years. This includes a wide range of solutions to improve healthcare for women across several female-specific conditions, including maternal, menstrual, pelvic and sexual health, fertility, menopause, and contraception, as well as many general health conditions that affect women disproportionately or differently (such as Osteoporosis or Cardiovascular Disease). This includes overcoming women's unequal access to healthcare, a major injustice in itself.

While it's still early days, my desktop research indicates that the underlying dynamics of FemTech are accelerating: public awareness, company formation, and funding are surging. Half the world's population are women, so this is a mega-trend, empowered by a deep-rooted sense of injustice.

I observed that increased female representation among researchers, inventors, investors, and founders could create more consumer-centric products and solutions that recognise and target women-specific healthcare needs. Indeed, the market is not just women consumers, but also payers and providers that seek better products and tools to engage more effectively with women end consumers.

FemTech solutions are not only achieving commercial success; they are contributing to the conditions for continued innovation. Because women are not just consumers but the primary healthcare decision-makers for themselves and their families, better health outcomes for women can lead to better results for society.

I was starting to see those missing pieces in my journey.

Women often think they need to gain the right skills, especially when it comes to information technology. My advice would be not to worry about that. I have never worked in information technology before, but that can make you more humble, ask better questions, manage specialists, and become a better entrepreneur. Because ultimately, being an entrepreneur is building a great team. It means I can embrace bringing in the best people and then letting them lead and contribute in their specialist areas. Male entrepreneurs often call this "standing on the shoulders of giants".

A key success factor is to have a strong purpose. As a founder entrepreneur, you must be passionate about your work and committed to your big audacious goal. There will always be tough times, and you must keep going through them. Be in charge of that change. I did this by founding my own consulting business and organising workshops and digital health conferences addressing Women-in-Health issues. We need to talk to enough women to know that this is a real problem and that the solutions could help us. You must develop a thick skin and focus on your goals.

This brings me back to the initial question at the beginning of this chapter.

How many of you would like to make a difference?

If so, find out as much as possible about the means that drive your passion and be very targeted. Know what product or service and what problem you want to solve. Entrepreneurs don't just come up with an idea; Shakespeare said in Twelfth Night, "Some are born great, some achieve greatness, and some have greatness thrust upon them." I think this applies to entrepreneurs and the problem they passionately work to solve.

From an innovation point of view, FemTech is an exciting opportunity. With FemTech, I will make that difference through my consulting business, a future start-up or supporting and empowering other female entrepreneurs. This is my passion and my life; that is what my heart and mind are driven by!

What about you? Are you willing to restart your life and reinvent your career?

ABOUT THE AUTHOR

NASHYA HAIDER

Nashya Haider (Innotech Consultants) is an internationally experienced (Europe, America and SE Asia) Program Manager within the Healthcare and Health-Tech industries and academic research environments. She is an executive and consultant, enthusiastic about promoting technology-driven business solutions.

Nashya focuses on internal innovation that drives better customer-facing business processes and external innovation that drives new product adoption with industry key opinion leaders.

She has a proven track record of implementing AI business growth strategies by establishing strong partnership networks, organising international conferences and training events, and developing programs and curricula.

Nashya is the Program Manager of complex projects involving interdepartmental and multidisciplinary stakeholder groups across ICT/AI, healthcare, health-tech and marketing functional areas.

You can connect with Nashya at:

✉ : nashyahaider@gmail.com

in : https://www.linkedin.com/in/nashya-haider-phd-mphil-2563423/

STORY SEVEN

My 20-Year Journey as a Migrant Domestic Worker

Armed with nothing but a strong purpose, determination and a dream.

One night, I sat on my bed, crying while packing my bags. The thought of being separated from my family for the first time breaks my heart, and the thought of going to an unfamiliar place terrifies me. I've heard many sad stories, and I can't help but wonder if I will survive and see my family again.

After what seems like forever, I've finished packing. I look at my four sleeping children and kiss them goodbye. With a heavy heart and tears in my eyes, I leave my family and embark on a journey into the unknown. Armed with nothing but a strong purpose, determination and a dream of giving my children a better future as a Migrant Domestic Worker (MDW)

Hailing from the Philippines, I got married when I was 18 and had three boys and a girl. Sadly, my marriage broke down after ten years. I was left with four small kids to support. I have no choice but to leave my kids behind and find a greener pasture. I came from a low-income family and had a challenging childhood. I don't want my kids to suffer the same fate, so I muster all my courage and go abroad to work.

In my first few years abroad, I had a hard time coping. I've faced some challenges of cultural differences, language barriers, homesickness and feeling isolated. I found it hard to adapt and fit in, I have had my fair share of good and bad employers. So I changed employers ten times in over 20 years. I've managed to finish contracts with five of them; with the rest, I had terminated my contract early.

I was verbally abused by one of them, even locked inside the house when they went out, and not given a day off for two years nor allowed to use the phone. I've communicated with my family through fortnightly letters. I was accused of theft by another employer. They threatened to call the police if I didn't admit I committed the crime. But I told the employer that I may just be a helper, but I am not stupid and will never admit something I didn't do. The law is fair and just and will not lock me up in jail without solid proof.

Another employer did not give me enough food and rest, and I was forced to sleep in the lounge area with a thin mattress with no pillow or blanket.

Yet another employer was verbally abusive. It started as early as three days after I joined them. I was scolded and shouted at over trivial issues, as trivial as the taxi I booked being either two minutes early or three minutes late. They wanted it at an exact time, and my employer was unwilling to compromise. I was scolded day in and day out. It was so loud and so frequent that our neighbours became alarmed.

Every time they saw me outside the house, they asked if I was ok and if I needed help. I politely declined the kind offer of help and told them I could manage. If there's any consolation, I was just verbally abused but never physically. That's my bottom line. If the employer lays their hands on me, I will contact the police straight away.

The downside of being a direct hire transfer is that I didn't have an agency to turn to. So I contacted the Ministry of Manpower (MOM) instead. When my then-employer found out that I complained about her, she compromised and signed my release papers. But not before shouting at me and saying, "You are the worst helper I have known in my entire life!" Although her words were insulting and hurtful, I didn't take them to heart. I just listened, apologised for the inconvenience I've caused and moved on.

Sometimes I cried to sleep and thought of just packing my bags and going home. But when I thought about my kids, who would suffer if I did this, I had to reconsider. Like every typical mother who loves their children dearly, I was willing to make sacrifices for their sake.

Bieng an introvert, so I don't have many friends despite working in Singapore for many years. I don't easily warm up to others and am picky about who I hang out with. I don't like socialising, so in my first few years in Singapore, I spent my days off at home, in the park or hanging out in the library and reading books.

I came across the Centre for Domestic Employees (CDE) and Uplifters through social media. At that time, I felt like my monotonous routine was suffocating me, so I was desperately trying to find ways to spend my free time more meaningfully.

I joined CDE as a volunteer in 2018 and joined Uplifters in the same year as a student under the guidance of the Uplifters Founder and CEO, Marie Kretz Di Meglio. I became a team leader a year later and eventually a Mentor.

Joining Uplifters as a Team Leader and Mentor shows my gratitude to Uplifters for helping me steer my life in the right direction. I used to have low self-esteem and was in endless debt no matter how I hard I tried to get out of it. But by applying the lessons I've learned in Uplifters, I've managed to get out of debt slowly and become more confident.

During my time in Uplifters as Team Leader, I spoke to different migrant women from different countries. Aside from discussing our lessons, we also shared the challenges we faced in our work and gave words of encouragement and tips that might be helpful to each other.

At first, I thought I had a tough life. But after speaking to other migrant women, I've realised that my difficulties are nothing compared to some of them. It is inspiring to hear that they remain hopeful despite going through a difficult life and believe things will get better in time. I've learned a lot, and I am truly grateful for that.

My 20 years working in Singapore might not have been all rosy, but it has its perks. I have had quite a lot of memorable experiences. I've been to places I never dreamed I would be able to go. Raising my four kids single-handedly is quite an achievement, too.

During my stay here, I completed short courses, like basic computer and computer electives, business management and a First Aid course at the Singapore Red Cross, all paid for by my previous employer. I've attended many workshops, both face-to-face and online.

While with another employer, I could travel to many countries, like Malaysia, Vietnam, Indonesia, Dubai, Abu Dhabi, Denmark, Sweden and Belgium.

Being an active volunteer, I expanded my network in Singapore and beyond and made new friends. I have also had the opportunity to meet fellow domestic helpers worldwide, in Hong Kong, Dubai, the Middle East, Europe, Africa and Singapore.

I also received awards, certificates of recognition and achievement and have been interviewed by the Philippine embassy and mainstream media in Singapore.

I managed to achieve some of my goals while supporting my kids and their education. All four of them are college graduates and have good jobs. My eldest and youngest sons are in the police force. My second son works in a financial company, and my third child, my only daughter, works in Europe. My kids and I managed to build a house of our own.

Being away from family over a long period isn't easy. It's physically and mentally exhausting. But I've managed to cope because I have a strong purpose and always remember my goal of leaving my family behind. The downside of having a strong character is that everyone assumes I am always ok and can battle every storm that comes my way.

Many of my fellow domestic helpers, especially those I've managed to help one way or another, thought I was unbreakable and would always be a strong support.

But no matter how strong I am, I'm still human. I also feel exhausted and need a shoulder to lean on from time to time.

What broke my strong mental resilience was when my mother passed away in June last year. Her passing hit me hard. She was my source of strength and inspiration. Her sacrifices, unconditional love and endless guidance, taught me how to face even the toughest challenge in life.

I used to have an annual home leave, but I couldn't go home for more than three years due to the pandemic.

I was looking forward to the opening of the borders so I could take my home leave. But sadly, before that time came, my mother passed away.

The grief of loss was so overwhelming, and in the process, I started withdrawing from society. I stopped my online classes halfway. I stopped taking my off days. I stayed away from social media, lost my appetite and couldn't sleep. Luckily, I had an empathetic employer.

She dragged me out of the dark pit I put myself into. I just broke down when she asked me how I was coping with my mother's passing. She gave me a two week break from work and told me to go out of home and socialise.

I forced myself back into the outside world. I started going out again and meeting friends, got back into social media, and signed up for Mental Health and Psychological First Aid workshops, and before I knew it, I was back on track.

I am grateful to my family, employer and the community I belong to for showing love, care and empathy during my darkest moments. I don't know what to do without them.

No one is an island. It's a cliche but true. No one is self-sufficient; at some point, we need to rely on others to get through life's challenges.

The CDE and Uplifters are the two NGOs I've joined as a volunteer. CDE focused on assisting distressed MDWs in Singapore. In comparison, Uplifters focuses more on money management and personal growth. I am happy to be in a community with a heart, a community that cares.

Life abroad can be really tough. But with a strong purpose in mind, patience, determination and a good social support network, any challenges will be manageable. To my fellow migrant women, when your determination wavers, remind yourself of your purpose in leaving your family behind. That will help you to stay focused and keep going.

In this life journey, we will be kicked and tossed like a soccer ball. But keep the faith, be strong and stay positive. Never give up! No matter how difficult the situation is now, it will get better. We must hold on to our dreams and believe in ourselves that we can do it. More importantly, pay attention not just to our physical health but to our mental health as well. Self-care is important. If we are mentally unstable, we cannot be productive at work. We need to care for ourselves first before we can take care of others.

I hope my life's story will inspire others.

ABOUT THE AUTHOR

EVELYN OBILLO

Evelyn Obillo is a Filipino migrant domestic worker in Singapore for the last 20 years, a CDE ambassador, Uplifters mentor and a mother of four.

She is an active NGO volunteer. Helping others is her passion. She assists fellow migrant women with their employment issues and integration into the community. She helps them not feel so alone and become happier so that their stay is more tolerable and fruitful. She is also helping Uplifters to facilitate their online classes and mentors the class team leaders.

Evelyn has a friendly, warm and straightforward personality. She is able to connect with her fellow migrant women and make them feel at ease to open up about their employment and personal issues as well as advising them on how to use social media. In her free time she conducts outreach programs and attends workshops that are beneficial to her.

You can connect with Evelyn at:

: Evelyn_singapore@hotmail.com

STORY EIGHT

My Global Journey: Family, Work and Travel

The best advice I can give is what worked for us: talk it out.

Sometimes I wonder why I always wanted to travel. It wasn't that I needed to leave because I was unhappy; I simply wanted to see and learn about different places and people.

And I am thrilled it happened this way. Thanks to this curiosity and a never-ending desire to learn, I obtained a global education, an MBA in Italy with an exchange in the US, a PhD in the UK, and lots of travel and international work. Most importantly, however, it helped me resolve a cross-cultural misunderstanding with my then-new boyfriend, now husband of 30 years and bring up two bilingual and cosmopolitan children!

Challenging Beginnings

I'd dreamed of seeing the world ever since I could remember. At age 14, I wanted to attend a school in Budapest, our capital city, which was about 180 km away from my hometown. My dear mum didn't think it was a good idea.

I finally made it to Budapest during my university years, but I also wanted to study abroad. This may not sound like a special dream, but I lived in Hungary – as many would refer to it – behind the Iron Curtain. I was not allowed to travel freely, and travelling to the "West" was possible but very limited.

You may wonder what I mean by the "West". Hungary was one of the countries that were put under the control of the Soviet

Union after the Second World War. We were part of Eastern Europe, and anything west of Hungary was considered the "Forbidden West" for us.

Here are some examples to give you a sense of how this felt.

I knew something was fundamentally wrong when I was able to go to the UK for a short trip and had to smuggle some history books home rather than bring them openly back to Hungary. I knew there was a good chance I would be kicked out of the university if the books were found in my luggage. I confess I was pretty scared during the border search.

A dear friend told me about how she managed to get to the US. You could apply to work in a summer camp with American children. There was a catch, however. You had to pay a $10 application fee, and in Hungary, at the time, we were not supposed to own "Western" currency. My parents managed to come by the dollars, and one Saturday morning, we all got into our Trabant (an old East German car) and deposited the money into an Austrian bank. This was how I managed to go for the first time to America.

Cross-Cultural Differences – Marriage and Children

Then, the world changed. Eastern Europe opened up, and I could secure full scholarships to study first in Italy, then the US and finally the UK. I was living my dream. I shouldn't forget to mention that in the meantime, I also married my wonderful English husband!

Marriage across cultures can last, but you do need to work at it. The best advice I can give is what worked for us: talk it out. Try to clarify whenever you feel there is a chance of misunderstanding or are unsure why your partner would say such a thing.

My now husband and I were working together in a small office, and according to company policy, you were not supposed to date a colleague. As the relationship was just starting, we kept it secret. One evening, a group of us went out for dinner in the hotel where he was staying. Dinner finished relatively early, but since it was a work day the next day, everyone went home afterwards.

When I got home, my husband called me. I told him I was tired but happy to meet for a drink. He then told me it was okay; we didn't need to meet, and we could always have a drink later in the week. And then wished me a "Good night". I wasn't sure what was happening. Didn't he like me after all? Why didn't he want to meet up? I was blaming myself for how this could happen to me. Why did I tell a man I wanted to meet him when he didn't? I didn't sleep very well that night.

The next morning he behaved as if nothing had happened, but I felt very awkward in the same office. A couple of hours passed, and we uttered a few niceties to each other, and then I couldn't take it anymore.

I went to his desk and asked straight out, "Can we please talk? I am confused. You are acting as if everything was fine, yet yesterday you didn't want to see me."

It was quite obvious from his reaction that he had no idea what I was talking about. We started chatting, and eventually, he said, "You said you were very tired, and I took it as a cue that you'd rather go to bed than go for a drink."

That was his interpretation. My sentence, however, wasn't meant as a cue. I simply stated how I felt physically. I still wanted to spend some time with him that evening.

Later on, I could understand the situation as I learnt about cultural differences. Most Hungarians are pretty direct, straightforward people and say things as they are. At the same time, most English people are more indirect, using a more diplomatic language. This difference was the key reason for our misunderstanding. Thankfully we talked about it. This incident taught us to clarify what we mean instead of assuming we know what the other person is saying.

We also had cultural differences in how we wanted to raise our children. Given my upbringing, I could have been a bit like the Asian "tiger moms", pushing for more and more academic achievement in subjects I deemed important for them. My husband, however, wanted to leave things up to the children's choice. I appreciated and liked this idea, so I adjusted my approach.

By having lots of conversations, admittedly leading at times to arguments, we found a way to manage our parenting roles. In the end, we raised two beautiful people who grew up internationally as third-culture kids and with great sensitivity to different cultures.

Women in Leadership Positions

In Hungary, we didn't overthink gender equality. The communist ideal - which we were supposed to follow but didn't - assumed equality among people. Our constitutional requirement also illustrated this: women AND men HAD to work. As a result, I grew up in an environment where all women worked unless they were on maternity leave.

Please note I am not claiming there was gender equality then or even today. Hungarian society is still quite macho in its outlook. However, since everyone had to work, some women eventually reached the top. My mum was one of these great ladies. She was in a leadership position in a bank for over 20 years.

Many things surprised me when I first lived abroad for a longer time. In Italy, I saw how lonely female leaders felt and how much harder they had to work than their male colleagues to prove they deserved to be in their positions. As I continued my journey and lived in different places, I saw how pervasive the issue of gender equality was, albeit with different flavours and nuances in every country.

"Women's voices are not heard in meetings," said my new friends in the US. In Switzerland, I learned that women couldn't vote until as recently as 1971! In Thailand, I was told how "normal" it was for men to be unfaithful. And the list and the learnings just went on!

Key Advice for Working Effectively Across Cultures

I started this chapter by saying that my dream was to travel and see different places and people. In addition to having a happy international family and fantastic travel, I have also been able to do work that I love. My present work, be it consulting, training or coaching, is about global, inclusive, female and cross-cultural leadership.

How did it all start? My job in a global accounting firm in Hungary made me realise it was not enough to be good at your profession if you want to work in an international environment. You also need to be culturally aware.

I was often asked to accompany our foreign managers to project debrief meetings where they would present the financial results and recommendations. Unfortunately, not all my colleagues recognised it would be a good idea to ask for the local people's opinion about these recommendations before presenting them to our clients.

So there I was, my young self, sitting in a meeting with a Hungarian general manager, even a government minister (as it was a time of significant economic, social and political change in Hungary, and we were hungry for foreign advice), and my colleague's recommendations didn't make sense in the Hungarian context.

The business environment was different, people's thinking was different, and the "Western" solutions simply didn't work. There I was, wanting to be loyal to my company and look intelligent to my fellow Hungarian counterparts. These very uncomfortable situations made me shift to pursuing global leadership.

Moving forward a few years, I worked on a leadership program at the IMD business school in Lausanne, Switzerland. The focus was not on global or cross-cultural leadership but on leading people in general. Then just two minutes before the end of the session, a participant asked, "I don't have time to attend a cross-cultural course, but I need some advice on how to become more effective when working with different nationalities. What would you say?"

At that time, I struggled to give a quick answer, but the question made me think. In the end, this is the general advice I came up with: *Be genuinely OPEN and RESPECTFUL, try to consciously LIMIT YOUR ASSUMPTIONS, practice PATIENCE and FLEXIBILITY, and be willing and able to SHIFT STYLES.*

This question and the many workshops I ran encouraged me to write a short practical book: The Culture Key between Asia and the West. It covers the essentials I believe everyone should be aware of, whether you are working abroad, in a multicultural office or are communicating via emails, phone calls, etc., with international colleagues.

Here are three of the most impactful cultural differences and a very quick tip for each:

> The biggest difference that causes perhaps the most frustration, derailed careers, and lost deals is whether we have a preference for a direct or indirect communication

style. This often creates negative perceptions, and since "perception is reality", these negative perceptions lead to negative consequences.

For those who prefer direct, straightforward communication, we should be more careful about using "hard" words, such as – must, have to, obviously, and now – which may sound aggressive to others.

For those who prefer a more indirect style, we should be aware that adding "I may be wrong, perhaps, should, could" to our sentences may sound like we lack self-confidence and knowledge to our direct colleagues.

Different cultures have different approaches to hierarchy and equality. To build an inclusive and "speaking up culture," you must consistently create that culture over time.

Another difference between cultures is the length of silence or gaps in conversation. Some of us need a gap before we feel it's appropriate to add our comments, others are quite happy without any gap, and some cultures don't even mind people overlapping each other. Once we become aware of this, we can observe our communication and should be able to create more balanced participation in meetings and in communication in general.

Thirty years on, I am happy and am living the dream. I have a wonderful international family dotted around the world, international work focusing on global, inclusive, female and cross-cultural leadership, and I am still learning something new every day.

ABOUT THE AUTHOR

DR. ZSUZSANNA TUNGLI

Dr. Zsuzsanna Tungli is an expert and passionate advocate of global and inclusive leadership, gender equality and cultural intelligence. Over the past 30 years, her work has spanned Asia, US and Europe in consulting, research and executive education.

She has designed and run most of her programs as the Managing Partner of Developing Global Leaders and as an invited faculty member at the following business schools: INSEAD, IMD, London Business School, University of St. Gallen, National University of Singapore and Singapore Management University.

She is the author of the books The Culture Key between Asia and the West (2020), and The Roadmap to Gender Equality in Organisations (forthcoming), and a regular speaker and facilitator at international conferences and company events. Zsuzsanna earned a PhD in international business at London Business School, UK, and an MBA at Bocconi University in Milan, Italy. With her first degree, she graduated as an economist from Corvinus University in Budapest, Hungary.

You can connect with Dr. Zsuzsanna at:

: ztungli@developinggloballeaders.com

: https://www.linkedin.com/in/zsuzsanna-tungli-ph-d-82a327/

: https://www.developinggloballeaders.com

STORY NINE

Navigating Constant Change as the Wounded Healer

We are constantly evolving, whether we realise it or not.

"Change is the Only Constant". It's a phrase I have learnt to believe is true despite my need for comfort and security and for the status quo to remain unchanged. Life goes on whether I want it to or not, and as it does, tidal waves resembling tsunamis have washed over me, bringing unrelenting change and the need to recalibrate myself and realign my life constantly. Marriage. Children. Chronic Illness. Divorce. I was unprepared for these changes and their impact and how my life would be utterly transformed, even beyond recognition at times.

When I got married at 26 in 1994, I started a new life in Singapore, having been born and bred in Malaysia. I spent a year abroad in the UK pursuing an MA in Linguistics and returned to marry the man who'd said he loved me and vowed to spend the rest of his life with me. We were, seemingly, the perfect couple.

He was an extremely busy professional, and I was a Researcher and later a Producer at the Singapore Broadcasting Corporation (SBC). I often joke about going from producing to reproducing since I left SBC in 1996 and had four children in seven years. I became a full-time stay home Mum, and I home-schooled for several years. I gave up my career as I stayed home with my beautiful children and watched them blossom, but in doing so, I lost my health.

It began during my first pregnancy when I started having gastrointestinal problems. It was regarded as hormonally induced due to the pregnancy and was left untreated. Unfortunately, I had retained the placenta after the delivery of my eldest son in 1996 and needed a D&C and antibiotics to treat the infection. My second pregnancy seven months later was exhausting, and the symptoms worsened and included low-grade fevers, joint pains and exhaustion.

When my second son was born in 1997, I struggled to breastfeed him and manage two young boys. Eventually, the symptoms got so bad that I was admitted to the hospital. Over the next couple of years, tests led to a diagnosis of Crohn's disease, an incurable, inflammatory disease of the digestive tract. I was 31 when I was diagnosed, and I finally got started on some medications that helped me a little. I had a daughter in 2002 and my youngest son in 2003. Sadly, my youngest son was also diagnosed with Crohn's disease when he was eight.

My late father passed away in 2009, and I was deeply affected by this loss. I was not close to him all my life because he had rejected and abandoned me as a child, but his death was a grievous blow to me, and I mourned the father I had never had. This stress exacerbated the disease and resulted in my needing surgery in 2010. It was a resection of my small intestine and removal of my gallbladder.

The disease had progressed and caused narrowings due to scarring from ongoing inflammation, so 14cms of my small intestine needed to be removed. In 2019, I needed surgery again due to stress from my divorce and further rejection and abandonment. I had an abscess and another 14cms of intestine removed. Stress, especially chronic stress, was not helpful.

Life with an incurable chronic illness is like a rollercoaster ride, and I don't like rollercoasters. You don't know when the ups and downs are coming and whether you'll make it over the next steep climb or survive a sharp drop. You just know that you must hang on, hang tight, scream along the way, and go with the flow of constant, unrelenting change.

When I often planned to do something with my life or family, the disease would pull the rug out from under my feet. The disease's flare-ups, followed by dormancy, and then flare-ups again, and all the while, you look normal on the outside, but there's a war being waged inside your body. It's hard for others to understand, especially if they are healthy.

You live with a terrible disease but get little understanding, compassion, or empathy, and it's the loneliest journey one can imagine. It's an autoimmune condition where the immune system attacks healthy cells. The primary treatment is immunosuppressants with side effects such as photosensitivity, mood swings, profound exhaustion, and frequent infections. You feel trapped between a rock and a hard place, with the disease tormenting you and the medications causing further problems.

All of this took a toll on my marriage. In addition to pursuing his high-powered career and succeeding, my ex-husband struggled to be truly present at home for our children and me. I needed his help as I faced profound fatigue and exhaustion, migraines, joint pain, colic pain, multiple loose stools, recurrent fever, photosensitivity, inflammation of my auditory nerves, early osteoarthritis, osteopenia, mood swings, perimenopausal symptoms, and quite unsurprisingly, depression.

Chronic illness is isolating, but I also felt neglected and left to worry about raising four children alone without the necessary emotional support and parental assistance from my ex-husband. I thought he was married to his work, and I was worried for my children while battling an exhausting chronic illness and struggling to find the proper medication with minimum side effects.

I struggled to manage my emotions and articulate my needs but found myself guilt-stricken, resentful, and angry. I needed help and begged for it, but no help was forthcoming, and I was alone in my struggles.

I broke my ankle in 2013 and was in a wheelchair for a few weeks, during which time my marriage ended. I felt used and thrown away as if my life was worthless and meant nothing to the man I loved. I wanted to die, but I realised that if I did, my children would be lost, so I ran back to my faith in God and sought to work on myself and be a better person, hoping it would save my marriage.

Unfortunately, it was too late, and I felt betrayed, rejected and abandoned. We filed for divorce in 2016, which was finalised in July 2017. I had just turned 50 in June, knowing then that I would be alone going forward.

Whatever happened to that young woman, full of life, top of her class, bright, bold and beautiful, who fell in love with the man of her dreams and then woke up years later to find herself in her worst nightmare? She was crushed. Totally and utterly annihilated. Her former self was gone; it had been diminishing over time as she gave away so much of herself to others that she no longer recognised herself.

What did my ex-husband want? What did the children need? Who was that strange person in the mirror? I was exhausted, grieving, and hurt. I was wounded, like a creature that lost a wing; I could no longer fly.

One of my favourite creatures is the butterfly. It's beautiful and catches the eye as it flutters by – bright, bold, beautiful. And yet, its origins are humble and relatively unremarkable. From a tiny pupa, a caterpillar emerges, devouring everything in sight until it's satiated and ready to spin its cocoon. In this cocoon, it slumbers, not anticipating its future or consciously knowing what is ahead. Utter annihilation awaits.

A complete metamorphosis from one state to another as the caterpillar's body liquefies and every cell in its body is changed over time. Eventually, a beautiful butterfly breaks forth from the chrysalis, and no one sees the horrific transformation the caterpillar has undergone. They only see a gorgeous butterfly, testing its wet wings, preparing to fly, to bring joy wherever it goes, and to thrill with its beautiful but short life. Utter destruction can lead to absolute beauty.

Metamorphosis is change at the deepest level when one gives in to the process and allows transformation without fighting it. We are constantly evolving, whether we realise it or not, and the challenge is to let it happen, to roll with the punches, to be self-aware of what we can learn from each moment, to survive, and somehow, to thrive. How are we evolving, in what direction, and what do we wish to become as we journey through painful moments in life?

As I journeyed through the years following the death of my marriage in 2013, I gave up some dreams, like finishing my PhD, and explored new horizons. I pursued my MA in Counselling in 2016 to train as a counsellor and to find new direction in my life. I felt that all the suffering I had endured, all the grief and sorrow I had felt, and the many tears I had shed were not, and should not, be in vain.

I refused to see my life as pointless, worthless or a throwaway. Instead, I drew upon my years of experience raising four children, volunteering with the chronically ill, and surviving heartbreak and divorce and decided that I could put all my lived experiences to good use.

My life would have meaning, it would be productive and valuable, and I would help others through my formal qualification as a counsellor. I started my counselling practice, "Patient Voices", and began seeing clients. I have received 19 five-star reviews from clients who have found help in facing their journeys of change and metamorphosis. I look forward to many more years of helping others make sense of their struggles and finding clarity in the chaos.

My compassion, understanding and ability to empathise are all born from my deep struggles, mainly on my own, through nights of deep despair. I know what it is like to feel heartbroken, hopeless, abandoned, rejected, betrayed, neglected, unloved, unwanted, unappreciated, lonely, isolated, weary, depressed, and physically ill. I also know what it is like to overcome, to find strength, to keep going, to rely on others, to remain vulnerable, to learn to trust again, to stay hopeful, to keep the faith, to be open to love despite the heartbreak, to forgive, and to be content, joyful and at peace.

I continue to work on my healing while recognising that I am a "wounded healer" who reaches out to others despite my own wounds. I struggle with lingering PTSD, anxiety over my future, and fears and insecurities from being an empty nester. No one is spared their perfect imperfections, and I have weaknesses and insecurities like anyone else. Yet one thing I have learnt is that "Change is the Only Constant" and that it's best not to keep searching for a perfect life written in stone but to love deeply, hold on lightly, let go, and genuinely appreciate each lived moment for itself as life unfolds. Go with the flow, don't fight it.

I want my life to be lived with the foreknowledge that I am continually evolving and that I can decide the direction of my evolution as I choose to grow to become a better person. I no longer fight change, resent loss, grieve when people leave, or hang on to anyone or anything. I welcome change, and I embrace new adventures, new people, and new horizons.

I pursue my highest self each day, recognising that sometimes I might have to die a thousand deaths in the cocoon to become a gorgeous butterfly over and over, but it is all worth it because I'm bright, bold, and beautiful, and I bring joy to others.

What change may be coming your way, and how will you face it, work through it, and emerge from it? What might you need to let go of, and what might you need to embrace in your life? What fears are holding you back as you enter a cocoon phase, and what vision of yourself do you see as the butterfly to be? How can you be a "wounded healer" and bring healing to those around you and to yourself?

About the Author

Pavitar Kaur Gill

Pavitar Kaur Gill has been a wife, mother, teacher, tv producer, researcher, and is currently a counsellor. She raised four children aged 26, 25, 20 and 19 while living with Crohn's Disease, and navigating life as a single mother.

Her interest in counselling stems from her experiences with parenting, chronic illness, and divorce, and from her desire to help others find their way through life's difficulties.

She holds degrees in English (BA, 1990) and Linguistics (MA, 1993) but is a lifelong learner and believes in expanding her knowledge base and skills.

Pavitar completed her MA in Counselling in 2019 and founded her counselling practice – "Patient Voices". She is pursuing an online MSc in Psychology and Neuroscience of Mental Health with King's College London and aims to graduate in 2024.

One of her many life mottos is "Change is the Only Constant" which has helped her roll with the many punches that life has thrown at her. Pavitar is truly a survivor.

You can connect with Pavitar at:

: https://www.linkedin.com/in/pavitarkaurgill

: www.patientvoicessg.com

: www.journeywithpavsky.blogspot.com

STORY TEN

Our Life, Our Journey

We only fail if we quit.

Everyone's journey is different, but deep down, at a cellular level, I knew that my life had to become better than the first card I was dealt.

Our experiences either turn us into victims or victors. My choice was not to play the victim; I would not live the life I did in my childhood. I would simply not allow this in my life's journey!

As a young child, I grew up in a violent and abusive home because of an alcoholic father. I saw my mother, a mother of three children, unable to leave him because she didn't have the money or was not educated enough to find work. We stayed through it all.

I know now that we must go through the dark days to know what the light feels like. We don't just become compassionate, kind, and empathetic towards others unless we have first felt that pain. My voice had the power to change the course of my life, and it needed to be heard.

When I was 12 years old, my father died suddenly, and we were left with nothing but the Italian Welfare Association to bring us food to help feed us. I remember watching them unpack this box of food onto our kitchen table. This was when I realised I needed to make it in my life against all odds, to be self-sufficient for myself and my family.

My brother used to tease me for wanting to be better. He'd laugh when he introduced me to his friends, as: "This is my sister Patty. She thinks she is Lady Di."

It wasn't for others or to be better than others; I wanted to be the best for myself. To do this, I had to forgive myself for apologising for being me and putting my needs first.

Along my journey, I learnt to never stay too long in an environment or head space that would eat into my soul. I felt my feelings for a while but ensured I moved on to more positive spaces.

I no longer allowed my light to be dimmed for others. I no longer tried to fit into a box that was never made for me to fit into in the first place.

We are meant to shine our light onto this world; we are meant to be different. This is what makes our world so beautiful. Just be you.

All I wanted to do as a young adult was to go to university and study to better myself, but, at the time, I had no choice but to survive. I held three jobs just to pay my rent with barely any money left for food, but I never felt sorry for myself. I knew that many people were suffering a lot more than I ever did.

Deep down, I knew life, and I would be okay. I just needed to stop doubting my worth.

I know now that each time I was rejected and doors closed, many more doors opened. It's life's way of simply redirecting us. I didn't allow myself to quit or feel defeated. I knew that hard work was going to get me to my destination.

I always made sure that when I started something, I finished it. We only fail if we quit, so always give it your best, no matter how hard it may seem.

I studied while I worked my way up from a Bookkeeper to eventually a Managing Director and a Trustee. I worked hard to learn business intelligence/technology from a career in finance and banking.

It wasn't easy, as a woman in corporate. I was paid a pittance compared to my male counterparts and always had to work ten times harder. I had to fight to have my voice heard in a board room full of men, but I ensured my voice was heard and that, as a woman, I would not go unseen. Perseverance was key.

Our voice is important too. Women must be heard and have the right to be treated with dignity and respect.

I say thank you every day that I was given the gift of being born in a country like Italy and that I grew up in South Africa, where women are free, have the right to work and study, and have the right to choose who to marry, what to wear around their heads and the right to dress freely. I am so grateful that my daughter gets to experience this freedom too.

My heart goes to all the women still fighting for their rights. I cannot comprehend this atrocity in this day and age.

Women with rights are asked questions like, "When are you getting married? When are you having children? What do you do for a living?" Yet there is so much more to life.

As human beings, we should strive to help others. We were put on this earth to help those that have no voice, those less fortunate that cannot fend for themselves.

Why don't we ask more questions like, "What makes you happy? What made you smile today? What small act of kindness can you do today?" I remember my interviews always went something like: "Are you single? When are you planning to get married? When are you thinking of having children? Do you have children? How old are they?"

This was to ensure they picked the candidate that interfered the least with their work schedule. I had never had the opportunity to be a stay-at-home mom. I needed to work and survive in a male-dominated environment that didn't care whether my kids were running a temperature, where only the bottom line mattered. It's a real struggle. Our head knows you need to bring in an income, but your heart breaks for your children.

I worked hard to ensure that my daughter and son never went without food or a roof over their heads or that they never felt the pain and fear I had felt as a child. I wanted their childhood to be a happy one, full of good memories. I wanted to give them the life they deserved.

Our families are our most important treasure. I want my children to know that they are seen and heard, I want them to know how loved they are and every day that I am thinking of them. Our priority in life is to find happiness. It feels hard, but it's possible.

What do people that are dying regret the most? They regret not taking that chance and not following their dreams. My brother tragically died of a brain tumour and spinal cancer. I would have given my brother the shirt off my back to ensure he had everything he needed to make him comfortable. I took care of him for seven and a half years. I can clearly remember the day he died. On that day, I vowed that I must live the life my brother never got to live.

Life is so precious and so short! Take those chances, go on those walks to clear your mind and soothe your soul when you need to, travel, make the big moves, and do everything you can to pursue your happiness.

Don't let life dim your light; keep going no matter what. Don't listen to the naysayers. My children know to never ask advice from those that never took chances in life and to be grateful for all they have. They grew up knowing there is always a way if you have the will and grit to pursue your dreams.

To this day, I keep levelling up, and I keep learning. I keep evolving so that my life becomes something I am proud of.

Make sure that your growth is so enormous that people have to get to know you again and again, and remember that positive thoughts create positive outcomes, be kind, be human and just keep smiling through the hard times. These, too, will pass.

A decade ago, I created a vision board with a picture of a house at the coast to ensure my children were moved out of Johannesburg, a dangerous crime-infested city we'd lived in. I proceeded to tell my mother that we were going to move to Knysna. I'll never forget her response: "How can you move? You will never find work in a small town by the coast. My friends say that only the rich live in Knysna. What are you thinking?"

My answer was clear and concise. I have never listened to the opinions of those who don't matter, and I certainly wasn't going to start now. I will find work, and we will move there soon. This is all I knew and believed in.

I didn't worry about the how but ensured I worked towards it. I remember looking for work and schools for my children, and within six months, I'd found a job as a Bank Manager at one of the local banks, and here we were in beautiful little Knysna.

This happens when we don't listen to those who have never dared to dream, even if they are in our close circle.

Believe that you can and you will. I dared to dream and worked towards it, even if this dream seemed so far-fetched at the time.

Fast forward a few years. We survived the pandemic, but my employer of almost eight years died of COVID in 2020. His wish was that I wind up his affairs should something ever happen to him. Still, his family left me fighting for my severance pay in the labour court to try to get away from not paying me what was legally due while I was in for major surgery—another plot twist in my life journey.

I could have easily buried my head in the sand, but instead decided to start my own consulting business. While consulting to an audit firm, I met an incredible team in Singapore. This, in turn, led me to become a Co-Founder of a company called Sofinaa (Social Finance Using Applied Analytics). Sofinaa uses artificial intelligence tools to measure the impact of social development to help the disadvantaged. Here I learnt artificial intelligence. Sofinaa can do good on a much larger scale, which I have always dreamt about – to serve a larger group of people worldwide.

Life sends people we need to cross paths with in due course.

My journey with Sofinaa allowed me to be a Mentor and Board Advisor for Y:Wait (Young Women in AI Technology) and YGI (Young Global Innovators) to inspire young women and youth everywhere. I was also one of many speakers worldwide at Womenverse, a webinar to motivate women worldwide.

Our lives are forever evolving, just surround yourself with people who want to do better in this world, and don't be scared to be with those more intelligent than you. It's how we grow.

The expert now was also once a beginner. Remember, too, that it's always a good time to change the course of your destiny!

Stop overthinking it.

Live your life, don't just exist in it. Be the master of your Destiny.

ABOUT THE AUTHOR

PATRIZIA BONANDINI

Patrizia Bonandini is the Managing Director/Owner of Bonandini Consulting, a company she founded after her last employer passed of COVID in 2020. In 2021, her company was awarded Top Women, Top Gender Empowered Company.

She is also the Co-Founder of Sofinaa (Social Finance using Applied Analytics), a company that uses AI tools to measure how effective organisations are in their social impact to help the disadvantaged.

She is a Mentor and Board Advisor to Y:WAIT (Young women in AI Technology). She was recently one of the speakers at Womenverse – a global event for young women.

She aspires to become a great global entrepreneur. Social and community development are so important to Patrizia as, she knows what it's like to have nothing and wants to do all she can to help those in need.

You can connect with Patrizia at:

: https://www.linkedin.com/in/patrizia-de-sousa-10799a4

: www.bonandiniconsulting.co.za

: https://myfinb.com/sofinaa

STORY ELEVEN

Per Aspera Ad Astra

(Through Hardships to the Stars)

Take note of what makes you happy, as it might be your childhood dream inviting you for a new adventure.

If anyone had told me when I was growing up in Siberia, Russia walking to school at -30 degrees Celsius, that I would end up head of my own longevity recruiting company, have an amazing corporate career in HR and data science on Wall Street, live between the United States and Hong Kong, travelling all over the globe with my partner, working with most amazing fintech and biotech entrepreneurs on the planet and travelling 75 countries to date, I would probably say that this is a dream and the dreamer is absolutely out of her mind. This is not possible, especially if you are born in a small town in the middle of nowhere!

Yes, I am a DREAMER! I'm a big-time dreamer who has imagined all my life as it is, visualised it and visualised it another 1,000 times till I've got where I wanted to be. Have I always been this way? No. But I've learnt how to dream big, not give up, work my ass off, be positive even when the entire world is falling apart, and believe when no one else believes in you. Well, against all odds, it did happen to me, a simple Siberian girl who is just like anyone else but had dreamt big and had the courage and determination not to give up and move forward, taking that extra step when everyone else was discouraged.

Did I ever think that I was special? No. I grew up in a middle-class family. My mom was a journalist, and my dad was a piano tuner. They were busy working, and I occupied myself with gymnastics, piano lessons, art school, friends and a bunch of other activities that led me to get only As and graduated high school with 99.9 % as a class captain with a bunch of medals earned in city Olympiads which I didn't really care about.

Sounds like a great story. Getting into university and living life, which did happen, but not as I imagined. My parents got divorced, and the family lost money due to the financial crisis in the late 90s. My mom managed to get away to the US by a lucky accident to work as a nanny, leaving her career behind to provide me with money while I was studying for my World Literature degree. As a result, I started living on my own at the age of 18.

Three years have passed, and I've got an opportunity to go to the United States via the "Work and Travel" program, getting my first real job ever in Wildwood, NJ, working as a maid in a hotel.

My mom was not in a position to support me when I arrived. I immediately got a second job and started selling T-shirts on the boardwalk in a local store, working 100 hours a week. That was the first and one of the best summers of my entire life! I still remember getting on that bus in Atlantic City with $100 in my pocket, not knowing if I had a hotel and a job when I arrived, eating hot dogs every day, and making tons of international friends while learning English.

When I first went to Manhattan, I was so impressed and drawn by the energy and power of the city that I immediately knew that this was love at first sight. I wanted to be a part of New York City. I wanted to own it, and I wanted to be there no matter what! But how? I didn't have money, and the rent was so expensive. I barely spoke English, had no education, and had a job as a housekeeper, but I had such a strong desire to walk Manhattan not like a tourist but as a native New Yorker. Suddenly, that unknown movie that I had seen once when I was a kid became reality. It became MY reality where I wanted to work on Wall Street, walking to work in my fancy suit and heels, living in a flat with amazing views of the Hudson River, knowing – I'd made it.

It did become my reality, but ten years later. It took me five years of living in the United States without work papers. Of course, you say you could return to Russia and then come back, but those times were not easy. I was already getting into my last year at the university in Russia, which might have been my last chance to get into the US. And I decided to take a risk staying without legal papers, even though it was very scary.

I moved to Brooklyn after my first summer in New Jersey, getting jobs for cash in different stores – as a waiter, pizza maker, dental receptionist, you name it. I probably worked 20 different jobs and know how to do it all. I survived, and I enjoyed it. I built a huge amount of resilience, and if I ever had to do it again, I know I could.

Finally, I got my green card, and the minute I had it, I was admitted into Baruch College in Manhattan to pursue a Finance and Operations degree. I graduated in three years instead of four while working full-time as a receptionist. The story became even more interesting – I cold-called the Morgan Stanley Wealth department, begging them to hire me as an intern and guess what? They hired me. Even in those days, it was a pretty bold thing to do, but I was unstoppable.

One year later, graduation day arrives – and there I was, a 30-year-old woman full of hopes and dreams, walking down Wall Street like I was born there. But, I had no idea what I wanted to do with my degree. Nevertheless, I was super eager to start working immediately as I had an aggressive 10-year career goal to become the CEO of my own company!

When I graduated in 2010, the market was bad, but against all odds, I got 35 interviews, two job offers and a tech recruiter gig. While interviewing, I finally realised what I wanted to do. I wanted to be that person across the table that was interviewing me, hiring the best people for the company, and listening to the real candidate's stories and their reasons to shine in life. This seemed like a DREAM job!

I set a new goal to become a star recruiter at the firm I was working for, and guess what? A year later, I became a Rookie of the Year 2011. Dreams kept coming true!

The real excitement and culmination of my "Wall Street vision" came in 2015. I'd already managed to work internally for Barclays Bank and Nasdaq OMX. Finally, I received a talent acquisition job working one block off Wall Street under the JP Morgan investment banking technology umbrella! It ended up being the best decision of my life to choose that job.

It was really fun "walking "my American dream on a leash every single day to work exactly how I imagined it – strolling along Wall Street slowly, in my black suit with a cup of coffee, recalling days when I was cleaning hotels in New Jersey and appreciating every single step. I will never forget how it felt those days – a smell of victory mixed with a great sense of accomplishment by working hard to pursue my dream no matter how hard it was and feeling grateful for living such a wonderful life in the United States.

I continued working harder and harder, took a Head of AI recruiting role on the agency search side and worked long hours to become one of the top producers in the firm's first year of employment. But with all this hard work, determination, long hours, and stressful projects, I finally understood that my life had become hell. I was overworked and stressed, started losing interest in New York City life, and simply wanted to get out.

The solution came to mind fast – I wanted to pursue my other dream of living as an ex-pat outside the US. As a result, I relocated to Hong Kong for a year to explore Asia and had one of the best years of my life working, travelling, and making new friends every day!

It was time to return to the US, and I thought about new steps. I was 37 and still wanted to be my own boss by 40. Well, the answer came to me very soon after returning to the US and seeing the doctor. I found out that I had to have an operation. That hit me hard. Why me, and why now?

By realising that my health was in danger, I suddenly knew that my life was not only about work but about experiencing happy moments with my family and friends, helping others and doing meaningful work. This was a life-changing event for me that made me rethink my values and future dreams.

As a result, I decided to join a life science recruiting firm as a partner. I hit another goal of being in the C-Suite in my late 30s, but with a new approach to life and work balance. Furthermore, I became very active in the longevity circles bumping into the modern anti-ageing theory stating that ageing is a disease and can be cured.

I really started enjoying my new job when I realised that a whole ecosystem of entrepreneurs and scientists focused on expanding healthy lifespans and our quality of life. I immediately saw an opportunity to start helping longevity-focused companies find talent.

A longevity mindset became a part of my DNA. I also reconsidered my lifestyle regime and started eating healthier, got into meditation and Pilates, and began building more meaningful relationships with others. I've realised that my new dream was to live a happy, stress-free life connecting with like-minded individuals focused on the same beliefs as I had. I was finally ready to take responsibility and become my own boss.

With that said, I left my job in October 2021 and opened my own recruiting company called Ai4Best. It happened a few months before I turned 41 and officially made my lifelong dream come true! I became a CEO and a Founder of the first longevity in mind-focused search firm where candidates and clients are served to live their full potential and healthy lifespan.

Ai4best's philosophy is to bring good for all individuals in the world by creating an amazing start-up community of entrepreneurs whose mantra is in the power of ethical use of AI and positive thinking blended with science and technology to unite the best talent globally.

I am very excited about this new chapter in my life, and while looking back today, I can say with confidence – LIVE YOUR DREAMS, PURSUE THEM VIGOROUSLY AND DON'T LISTEN TO ANYONE! Only you truly know what you can achieve. There will always be people telling you that you are unreasonable, that you won't be able to accomplish it, and that there are people out there who are smarter, better educated, better looking, etc. And, my favourite – be realistic! But how is their reality relevant to your reality, to your dreams, where you are headed and what you are capable of?

You need to step back for a moment, breathe in, and listen to your heart. When you are on the right path, excited, and living the moment, you will know it. You'll have butterflies in your stomach, and your gut will tell you – do it – NOW.

It's like falling in love – when you know, you know it right away. If you do happen to catch this feeling, don't let it fly away and really take note of what makes you happy, as it might just be your childhood dream inviting you for a new adventure.

ABOUT THE AUTHOR

ELENA LIAPOUNOVA

Elena Liapounova was born in snowy Siberia and raised and lived in the US and Asia. She has built her career on Wall Street in recruiting, working with major banks, hedge funds, biotech companies, and VCs.

Having come to the US with only $100 in her pocket and working her way through college. AI and technology have become her bread and butter while building C-suite teams – her true passion. Fascinated by the recent technology and scientific discoveries, she decided to launch her own global search firm.

Elena's resilience, grit, determination, and positive attitude set her apart and are the reason for becoming one of the few female recruiting firm founders in the world.

Elena believes anything is possible! Her mantra is, "If I can do it, then anyone can do it." She dreams of living a happy long life filled with joy.

You can connect with Elena at:

✉ : elena@ai4best.com

in : https://www.linkedin.com/in/elenaliapounova/

🌐 : www.ai4best.com

STORY TWELVE

Perseverance, Resilience, Empowerment

Tools to Create a Resilient Mindset

You do whatever it takes. I read this in one of the books about having cancer my husband had picked up during the time I was having chemo treatment for brain cancer.

I remember reading the quote by Mark Anthony –

"And one day she discovered that she was fierce and strong, and full of fire and that not even she could hold herself back because her passion burned brighter than her fears."

I thought, "Yes, I am strong, and I have a burning desire to live, and I will do whatever it takes to live." Which I did. And the journey to get my books to millions of children has had many challenges, but I will never give up.

I am very grateful and honoured to share my story with you.

I hope you gain some insights and ideas that move you forward and upward, empowering you to persevere. I have learned that perseverance creates resilience which leads to empowerment.

In 2008 I lost my memory and was diagnosed with brain cancer.

I had been sick ever since moving to Hong Kong. Pneumonia, shingles, fluid in my lungs, and sores in my mouth caused me to lose a lot of weight and then I had double vision. The next step my husband thought was for me to see an immunologist.

After the double vision cleared, we went on a holiday to Bali.

On the plane ride home, I was asleep doing the funky chicken. My husband thought it was strange, but we had been up very early to get the plane home, so he thought I was overtired.

The day we arrived home in Hong Kong, we went to pick up some groceries. I received a phone call from my girlfriend and talked briefly with her. After I hung up, my husband, David, asked me what she had been up to. My reply was, "I don't know".

I then got another call, and after I hung up, my husband asked me, "Do you realise you asked the same question repeatedly?"

I did not. He was concerned and took me back to the doctor we had seen for the double vision, who put me on steroids.

The oncologist saw I was back in the hospital and said to stop the steroids now that I had been put on. It was critical to do diagnostic tests first to see why I had double vision. Because I had cancer when I was 14 years old, a diagnosis was paramount for the proper treatment.

The diagnosis came back as primary central nervous system lymphoma. Due to my memory loss, my husband had to deal with this. I remembered what we were told then but did not remember afterwards.

I had eight cycles of industrial-strength chemo that started immediately after the diagnosis. The chemo treatment, along with steroids, took over six months. Due to memory loss, I totally lost my confidence. I would get lost in our tiny plaza. So I did not go anywhere by myself for a long time.

My husband went to work every day even though they told him not to and just take care of his wife. But he continued to go to work every day and came to the hospital for the six days I was in each time. He would be the one to answer what was going on when people asked me, as I couldn't due to memory loss.

Courage: The courage to be strong. I cried every time my husband would leave in the evening when I was in the hospital. After getting my memory back, I thought, "Oh, I can't do that to him, as I know he already has so much to deal with". So after he kissed me, I waited until he was down the hall before my tears started.

As I regained my memory, I became afraid of dying. I told my husband because this was important to get it out of my mind where it could manifest into a bigger issue. I could share with him, which made me feel better. I also decided that "die" was just a word someone created, so I changed the word to transformation. This made me feel much more relaxed.

Triumph: Through this journey, I wrote about what I was going through, which has resulted in 22 children's books about the funny things that occurred during my treatment. I have also written four books from the adult perspective as well.

What Can Others Learn?

Having tools/ideas helped to shift my energy into a higher, more beneficial vibration. Choosing to take on my treatment, meditation, prayer, supplements, support and a will to live created a space for me to conquer the many illnesses I have had.

Kindness: Asking the people in my everyday life how they are and thanking them for the service they provided.

Who is inspiring? Many people are. We all have a story to share to support, empower and lift others to be the best they can be.

The real hero is my husband for being by my side through my many illnesses.

As well as my mom. She flew out right away to be with me for my first chemo treatment and two other treatments.

All of my incredible doctors, nurses and support staff dedicated to my return to complete health are heroes.

While I was in the hospital for my heart surgery, one nurse, in particular, felt comfortable sharing her husband's health issues after I shared my story with her. I am so grateful that this led her to do so. Sharing my story helped her immensely.

Tools I Used to Remain In or Return To a Place of Calmness

Because I had utilised and created tools, ideas and thoughts to sustain me during my illness, I have these to draw from in other situations.

I changed words that scared me and meditated every day on health. I prayed with my husband every night, creating centring and balance for us. I focused on living and having plans for the future. And I wrote the books that have given me a focus as I realised I had been put on this earth to help create a world without cancer.

Sharing: Sharing my story is important, and I do so regularly when I meet people. It helped me regain my confidence after losing my memory. In many ways, by sharing your story, you will impact many people. People may gain something from your story because you never know what they are going through, and what you have shared might be that pearl of wisdom that opens a door for them to see an opportunity or a new way to see the situation. I know, as this has happened many times. It is also beneficial for the people who are the caregivers to have support and be able to manage whatever stress or worries they have. Having someone to talk with, such as a friend or colleague or someone who has been through a similar situation, is so important. This is relevant to both adults and children.

When I read my books to children and their parents, I always tell them anyone can write a book if they want to. They can write about experiences they have had in their everyday lives. This is a way of empowering them.

I found that my books have not only helped kids with physical illnesses but have also greatly impacted kids with mental illnesses. For example, two children had both not wanted to live anymore. But after I shared my story and read my books, they both changed their minds. That is something to be very grateful for.

Creating tools that work to increase your mental strength and uplift you is a powerful way to gain empowerment and create a resilient mindset.

Being authentic, real and genuine and coming from a place of sharing to support and help others makes people feel they can gain something from you.

Perseverance is the key. Small steps or things done every day will move you towards your goal. My goal was to be in remission when I had brain cancer and to return to a state of health. I achieved this mentally and physically and then had to achieve it again after having the mastectomy and heart surgery in 2020.

Many people have told me that sharing my story/journey with them has been instrumental in supporting them with their own lives.

Tenacity: Persevering in my journey has resulted in the 22 children's books I have written about the funny things that occurred during my chemo treatment to make children and their parents laugh. I donate 50% of my net profits to cancer prevention, research and cure. Finding the positive and the benefit of what you have experienced can bring a whole new perspective to your life.

Steps or Changes You Can Make in Your Life

I say to people, when I share my books, they are all about me, but they have nothing to do with me. They are all about making children and their parents laugh.

It is a choice to choose to respond or react.

Talking to others to get what you are thinking about out of your head/thoughts.

Taking a deep breath and releasing it is calming.

And God/the Universe does not give us anything we can't handle.

Asking and accepting help/support from others creates a team.

Create affirmations to say every day that gives you strength.

Let other people feel that they can do whatever it takes. They can put one foot in front of another. They can ask for help. They can be scared. Then they can shift into feeling empowered and grateful. It is truly an honour to share what we have been through and experienced.

People have told me that I have inspired them, which I am truly grateful for. I would not wish anyone to go through what I have to gain increased awareness, but choosing to share our stories and giving to others through that experience creates a powerful outcome. We all have a journey that will benefit someone when shared. Find a way to step into your greatness and create it if you have a passion.

Creating Resilience

Resilience is an all-powerful tool that can be created by taking the following steps:

Focus on the good and the positive.

Address the negative and not-so-nice things to release them from your body and mind.

Find things about your situation that are funny, inspiring and interesting.

Listen to your language - I can't or I can.

Take on your power. This will also empower you.

Be kind to yourself.

You can choose how you feel, how you think, and what you create.

You choose your attitude.

Love yourself.

Although my journey has been challenging, it has been gratifying to know that I have so many opportunities and avenues to get my story and experiences out to more people. In doing so, I can lift them and provide a space for them to expand and express and increase their awareness of themselves and the world.

ABOUT THE AUTHOR

SANDRA ROE

Sandra Roe is a Canadian-born author now living in Hong Kong. Her nickname is "The Princess".

She has had cancer four times, major heart surgery, double pneumonia along with many other health issues.

Sandra had eight cycles of industrial-strength chemo over six months when she was diagnosed with CNS Lymphoma - brain cancer. After the chemo treatment, she wrote 15 children's books. The first book she wrote is called "The Farting Princess". Sandra has now written 22 children's books about funny things that occurred during her chemo treatment for brain cancer, as well as when she had a mastectomy and reconstruction for breast cancer and major heart surgery.

Sandra wrote her books to make children and their parents laugh as laughter is the best medicine. She donates 50% of her net profits to cancer research, prevention and cure.

She has lived in Hong Kong with her husband for 17 years.

You can connect with Sandra at:

✉ : sroeglobal@gmail.com

🌐 : www.adventuresoftheprincess.com

in : https://www.linkedin.com/in/sandra-roe-7ba6947/

STORY THIRTEEN

Showing Up

What would you do if you were not afraid?

My manager has called me to his office.

"You have been nominated to participate in the company Leadership Program. It is a long-term investment made in employees showing the potential to take on a management position one day. I would like to send you there, but I don't know if that is a good idea. You are 28 years old, and… as you want to have kids… I don't think this could work.

I felt my blood freeze in my veins. What was he talking about? I could not believe that in 2018, such discrimination could still happen.

"I am not sure I understand what you mean. Can you explain further?"

"Well, it is a nine-month program held in three countries, and only 21 participants are allowed yearly. We can't afford to invest in people who could drop out."

I realised what was happening. I took a deep breath and looked straight into his eyes.

"If you are happy with the quality of my work and my professionalism so far, I would like you to stop making decisions for me based on the assumption that I want to have children and ask you to add my name to the participant's list.

A long silence filled the room. I stood up and left, shaking like a leaf.

The unfairness of the situation was so obvious. It was happening before me, and what could I do about it? I had no one to look for and explain the situation to, only men being managers. I felt so frustrated and powerless. My future depended completely on the goodwill of a manager who was about to decide the direction of my career.

Frustration led me to join a women's business association as I was determined to seek help and know how to answer better next time. During one of the social events I attended, the help I desperately sought arrived in the form of a book recommended by one of my new friends. I still remember her whispering to me during a gathering: "You should read Lean In by Sheryl Sandberg.

No sooner said than done, I remember climbing the stairs of the Kinokuniya bookshop in Singapore and getting myself a copy the next day. One question Sheryl raised in the book kept haunting me: "What would you do if you weren't afraid?

Six months after that discussion with my manager, on a Friday afternoon, I was packing my suitcase and about to fly on holiday when I received a call from him.

"The next leadership program session starts on Monday. A participant just cancelled. So, I thought of asking you to take the free spot. But as I know you are on holiday next week, I assume you cannot make it either".

This was so unexpected. I had no time to read the briefing documents and prepare myself. Maybe the best thing would be to say no and wait for the next session.

I was about to reject the offer when Sheryl's question came back to my mind. "What would you do if you were not afraid?" At this moment, all came clear: I would invite myself to the table.

I calmly replied: "I'll be there on Monday."

When announcing to colleagues in the office that I was skipping holidays to attend professional training instead, some told me that I was only invited to join because of the quotas.

Would that comment have been said to a man my age, invited to make his next career move?

I showed up on the first day. A quick observation made things a bit more obvious: out of 21 participants, seven were women. I have never been a math genius, but still, I could count a very net 33% of women. Right in the bull's eye of the one-third quota.

I started to integrate "counting" as a habit that day. In any meeting I go to, I count the number of women in the room. On any organisational chart I see, I count the women managers. When watching a movie, I count: how many women are in the cast? Have a main role? How many were in the production or technical roles?

Counting is the best way to document misrepresentation with facts. It's data. It's tangible, and it's not refutable.

So, remembering Sheryl's book, I made a big decision at this stage. Even if a one-third women quota brought me there, I decided I still deserved the spot in the name of all women's misrepresentation. And if a quota brought me there, I would prove to them that my talent and hard work would keep me there.

After three days of intensive assessment done by business and HR professionals, I was told that I was one of the top performers in the cohort.

That day I decided another thing for myself. I will never let anyone's opinion dictate what is good or not for me. For many years, I was convinced that others knew better. Starting now, I will never let anyone influence my critical mind and tell me what is achievable. And if I deserved to be here or not.

From that day on, I decided to stand as far away as possible from what was expected of me and stand as close as possible to what I consider appropriate for my own standards.

Years later, I gave my resignation letter to my employer and decided to start my own business as a sales trainer in Germany. By then, I had learned that you only need one first customer to get started. If you wait to have six months of orders before starting your own business, you will never do it. One step after the other. But just start somewhere.

When my first deal was signed, I had to rush to create a company. After working enough time in Germany, I was allowed unemployment benefits and could use that to create a company. To access it and as part of the normal procedure, I got connected to a business coach to support me in writing a business plan in German before submitting it to a committee in charge of evaluating the reliability of the project. Without their approval, I could risk losing the financial help I needed to get started.

"Your business plan is way too ambitious for a first year. You need to lower it if you want to get the help of the state."

At this point, I realised again how ridiculous the situation was. I felt desperate and hopeless. What message did this send to me? As a woman, you can dream of starting your own business, but you will have to struggle twice as much as a man of the same age.

I thought of all the women who had hit similar walls before me. A 2020 report from the World Bank Gender Data Portal states that women are under-represented in entrepreneurship, as only one business out of three is owned by women worldwide. One of the reasons for this is that women face greater challenges in accessing financial services than men.

I couldn't help but make a parallel to Virginia Woolf and her book A Room of One's Own, published in 1929, as she explains why her generation counted very few women writers. To be able to write, she observed that women needed to rely on three pillars:

Time

Money

A room not to be disturbed.

Let's say that at this point in time, women were not allowed to work without asking permission from their male representatives, nor even have the right to access proper education. So, they basically could rarely get access to the three pillars.

Roadblocks to women's development have always been part of the journey. And if today the opportunity gap is considerably reduced, roadblocks are still paving the way in entrepreneurship.

As Virginia reflected on what was most needed to write a book, I reflected on what was needed to start a company. Time to focus is still a must, as well as money to get started. I also learned that the environment you evolve in has a bit of an impact. Most successful women entrepreneurs say their success rate increases when family and partners support them.

Looking at my situation, I thought I could directly influence Time and Environment from the three pillars. But not access to funding. This again depended on external factors, and I might not have the same chances as a man in a similar situation. What option did I have? Should I just give up and go back to look for an employed position? All seemed to be pointing towards that direction.

I thought of all women who decided to go backwards because of social and family pressure, lack of self-confidence and financial support. I then thought of those who decided to stick to their vision. Who did I want to be? I reminded myself of my code of conduct: do not let anyone decide for you what you can do or not. Decide that it is possible, and you will find a way to make it possible. I was convinced that my business plan was solid and realistic. I stuck to my plan and still submitted it to the start-up committee.

A few weeks later, I received a letter. The business plan got approved, and I received financial support to help me during the first year of setting up my company. Ignoring pessimistic opinions saved me from regretting not giving it a try.

And after a year of running my own business, I over-achieved the so-called "too ambitious" turnover forecast by 100%.

My Personal Code of Conduct

Remember that:

It is ok not to have any idea of how to do something or how to handle a situation. Get used to the idea of learning as you go.

Whatever happens, you can trust that you can find the resources you need to make it work.

You can't always anticipate everything. Making plans is great, but the probability that they will change is very high. The best opportunities are not predictable.

Plans are useful to reach your goals, but don't obsess about them. Use plans to your advantage: be flexible enough to adapt your plans but firm enough not to compromise your objectives.

You define your standards. You are the CEO of your life, and only you should have the power to decide what is good for you. What you are capable of or not. Who will stay in your immediate environment or not?

Each time you doubt your ability to do something, ask yourself if you would be ok with letting someone you don't admire do it.

When you feel scared about something, your internal belief system is tricking you. Fear is a normal reaction you can interpret as a signal that this is exactly what you must do. Choose to improve by going out of your comfort zone as often as possible.

You should not dismiss yourself out of fear. Show up. Even when feeling unprepared or not ready. Just show up!

Other women need you. Be the role model you wish you would have had.

People's opinions are not facts. Separate what they say from what you think. Ask yourself: "Are their comments helping me to achieve my goals?"

Whatever you choose not to do has a cost – the cost of inaction. What will happen if you don't do it? If you don't make THAT important decision?

There is always a way to turn what can appear to be a disadvantage into an advantage. The more people underestimate you, the more you can surprise them.

The most powerful question you need to ask yourself when feeling lost is, "What would I do if I were not afraid?"

I have no doubts that you know exactly what!

ABOUT THE AUTHOR

JULIETTE LEDOUX

Juliette Ledoux started doing Sales Training and Consulting as a freelancer, delivering Proactive Sales and Customer-centric Workshops after spending 10 years in Business Development. During that time, she worked on four different continents (South America, Africa, Asia and Europe) in the process engineering industry.

Her mission is to equip engineers with key techniques to improve their sales and business development skills. Her pragmatic approach uses a mix of soft and hard skills, such as situational intelligence and active listening.

The workshops are specifically designed for Technology experts, Field Service Engineers and Sales Area Engineers to generate new customer leads as well as increase customer loyalty to secure repeatable sales for a growing order intake. Her workshops are conducted in English, French and German.

After living four years in Singapore, Juliette now lives in Cologne, Germany, where she co-founded The Sparkle Academy GmbH.

You can connect with Juliette at:

✉ : jl@julietteledoux.com

in : https://www.linkedin.com/in/julietteledouxsalestrainer/

STORY FOURTEEN

The Magic Ring

I imagined I did have a magic ring
that could help everyone's dreams come true.

As the sun sets on a sunny winter's day in December 2022, I finish rereading a chapter called "Finding your voice" and close the book. The final sentences from the book, *Impactful Leadership* remind me reassuringly, "...you have discovered or rediscovered your true, essential voice through the exercises and stories in this chapter. You have befriended your voice and even begun to expand and stretch its capacity beyond its comfort zone... to get your essential voice heard."

I smile, comforted by the familiar words and the deep knowledge that they have supported many others to realise their potential.

I hear the faint lyrical echo of a children's poem that goes something like this.

"If I had a magic ring, I'd tell you what I'd do.
I'd wish a wish for everyone.
I'd wish a wish for you.
So maybe you can tell me, what you would like to wish for,
so I can use my magic ring to help your wish come true..."

Recalling the poem at dusk reminds me of two truths. Life is magical. My life is a miracle. I came to these conclusions at a young age, which has made all the difference. These beliefs morphed into a life purpose, to be a "catalyst" for others' potential.

I have had the privilege of living this every day for more than thirty years as a leadership coach and trainer. Annually, I complete a "check-in" on what being a catalyst means and how this can be expressed moving into a new year. I do not always have clear answers, but I always feel anchored. Being a catalyst ignites visions and plans to be in service and make a difference for an inclusive, leadership voice in the world.

One such checkpoint in 2014 fuelled me with a desire to capture and celebrate the success stories of people with whom I had worked and who had found their professional leadership voices. From the start of my career, I soon realised that most people are simply not heard. What stops them is a combination of limiting and negative self-beliefs, "confidence leaks", internal blocks, underdeveloped skills, and external obstacles. I created a four-step model to help emerging leaders find their uniqueness and demonstrate authentic leadership impact. The CABI™ model was proven across many cultures and corporations throughout Asia, Europe, and North America.

I began writing the book, I*mpactful Leadership: Unlock your power with CABI™*. Over the next seven years, I wrote (and rewrote) some stories from thousands of professionals who used the transformational steps of my model as a direct pathway to discovering their leadership voice.

CABI™ is an acronym that stands for the four essential components of having and projecting authentic, present and impactful leadership at any time, on any forum or with any stakeholder. C stands for both Confidence and Courage and how to access inner confidence and courage whenever needed. A is for Articulating with Impact and how to powerfully align one's inner world with the outer world to be a great communicator. B stands for Branding and how to create and live a professional reputation that aligns with one's values. I stands for Inquiry, which is adopting an attitude of curiosity to navigate any unexpected situation effortlessly.

While writing the first manuscript, my book coach asked me the following questions. "What about your story, Gina? Why are you so passionate and insightful on this topic? When did you first find your voice?" I deftly side-stepped these questions by replying, "It's what I trained to do" or "It's not about me. It's about capturing other people's stories. Their challenges. Their courage. Their dreams and accomplishments". The first manuscript did not include any of my stories. Even in the first chapters, "Finding your voice", "Am I a Leader," and "Confidence and Courage", I argued that there were better stories.

One day I received a testimonial from a client who had used CABI™ principles with her team and her children. I realised two things. First, the model is more than a pathway to leadership used only by professionals. The model speaks to the essence of being human. The evolving desire for expression and to be heard and seen, regardless of age, gender, education, economic status, culture or personality.

Second, I faced the truth that it is at the heart of my collective experiences and has a worthy place.

Today I share with you why "befriending" one's voice is the first essential step to having a voice in the world. At the age of six, I decided to stop talking. I lost my voice until I turned twelve.

Lessons 1 and 2: Your voice is not always popular. Others can use their voice and authority to eclipse yours.

At the age of five, I believed life was magical and filled with wonder. I lived like Mark Twain wrote, "*They did not know it was impossible, so they did it.*" I loved books and wanted to write. Noticing a typewriter, I taught myself to type one finger and letter at a time. I created, typed up and illustrated a story about a magic mermaid. When the teacher held up my "book" as a great example, I sat straight, hoping she knew it was me. Then I heard her say, "Of course, a parent must have done this as no child in Grade 1 could do this". I shrank and did not say anything.

The following year in my second school year, I turned six. There was great excitement as the school prepared for the musical production of Hans Christian Anderson's stories. I asked my teacher if I could participate in the musical. Her reply was an unequivocal NO. I was too young. I found a copy of the songbook and learned all the songs, especially the *Ugly Duckling*. I tried again, showing her my young acting skills.

The teacher laughed and said that Grade 2 students could only watch the production. Seeing my disappointment, she sent a letter to my mum suggesting that I enter the national Eisteddfod poetry section. I learned the *Magic Ring* poem by heart. I recall being on stage, knees knocking, stunned by the spotlight and all those eyes. I imagined I did have a magic ring that could help everyone's dreams come true. I recited the poem and received an award. My mother wept.

I was unprepared for the consequences of having a voice on

a public stage. Classmates teased me. I was uncomfortable with the attention received from teachers.

At the same time, I became aware of the ongoing domestic violence by my father on my mother.

When he found out that my mother had taken the entry fee money and entered me without his permission, the ensuing punishment was swift and prolonged. I recall pleading with her to report the abuse to the police. She did. I still remember the sound of clinking whiskey glasses as the police sat in the lounge with my father and laughed about how women should be kept in their place.

I quickly learned that having a voice was dangerous. A short while after that, my mother told me to secretly pack a small bag with only one book and a toy. One morning after my father left the house, she bundled me and my younger brother and sister into a car, and we ran away.

I changed schools seven times between the ages of six and twelve. Each change cemented my silence. My father would use his power and influence to trace us and persuade my mother to return, threatening to separate us from her. I quietened, even more, thinking that if no one knew, I could hide the shame and help to protect my mother, sister and brother.

Lessons 3 and 4: Accessing your voice feeds your courage. Your voice is most powerful and authentic when you express your truth.

I rarely spoke, but my energy and curiosity, common for six to eleven-year-olds, could not be suppressed. I read. I wrote. I observed. I walked and talked to the trees. I trawled through any book I could find.

Libraries were my friend. I plucked up the courage to borrow books and encyclopaedias from teachers. I read stories about people and communities who had beaten the odds. I read mysteries, adventure and travel stories.

Learning how the world worked and did not work, I created a context to make sense of my life. I kept a diary. It was as if writing a daily, chronological account of my days would reveal a hidden meaning. I collected discarded woman's magazines and created picture scrapbooks, categorised into topics like fashion, travel, dream homes and contentious issues.

I observed trends, historical pathways, tragedies and miracles. I began to see evidence that our family beat some gruesome statistics in adverse circumstances, poverty and the constant threat of domestic, political and social violence. Despite the veil of fear, I also experienced joy, love and learning.

At the age of twelve, I started the seventh school, and my father passed away from alcohol-related diseases. I experienced the veil of fear lifting. Our lives could finally begin. Throughout my teens, I gradually began to "befriend" my voice through sports. Playing individual sports like swimming and athletics boosted my confidence, teaching me the power of making decisions. Playing team sports provided my first experience that my voice could influence the game and outcomes.

Lesson 5: Your voice is a conduit to help others find their voice.

At sixteen, I finally made a bold and audacious statement. I began to state clearly and unapologetically, "I want to go to university". Despite all the impossibilities, I did obtain a bursary. The country was in a state of emergency. "Detention without trial" was a daily occurrence for anyone who spoke against an oppressive government. Student rallies and access to human-right activists were easy. As a History and Psychology student, the campus environment demanded that I use my voice. At the age of nineteen, I took on student representative committee roles.

I found my professional trainer's voice in my first job in 1991 as a distance-learning trainer for a bank's training college. I wrote self-study training courses supporting 35,000 employees. The country was having its voice heard for the first time. Nelson Mandela was released, and South Africa was preparing for its first democratic elections.

By the end of my first year, I had noticed several things. First, the departments and functions were silos. Second, very few staff had any voice. Third, the most stimulating conversations took place informally. There was little knowledge-sharing or communication between them. Suspicion permeated.

I felt afraid and compelled to do something. I developed a relationship with three colleagues from very different backgrounds. We found our collective voice by publishing a staff newsletter called Indaba Zethu, 'Our Story' in Zulu*. We interviewed a range of people across functions, departments, and levels, gathering different perspectives on diverse topics. We printed the stories of invisible people.

Our voice wasn't always popular. I was sworn at, screamed at and publicly confronted. In those moments of shock and fear, I would recall the lessons learned - your voice is not always popular; others will use their authority to eclipse yours; accessing your voice will give you the courage to claim your power and express your truth. Taking a deep breath, I'd focus on the purpose of the newsletter. I learned to seek support, quickly escalate and hold managers accountable for sponsoring diverse, collective voices.

My first job story taught me that many channels exist to express the essence of who you are. Everyone has many voices. My training voice expressed my professional training skills. My professional voice found ways to be heard in a hierarchical and patriarchal corporate environment. Recently these defining early career moments are in my book under the chapter EMERGING: "Finding Your Voice".

My wish is that my origin story shows you that the real and valid barriers to your voice, like language, economics, gender, education, situation, role or circumstance, are no match for your essential essence and the magic of you.

Choose to use your voice for the good of others, and you will find that your voice is all-powerful and can create the miracles of your magical life.

ABOUT THE AUTHOR

GINA MARESCIA

Gina Marescia's purpose is to be a catalyst. Since 1990 Gina has practised as a transformational leadership consultant, coach, and organisational psychologist. She has lived this purpose since her teens growing up in Apartheid South Africa and for the past thirty years as a global leadership coach and trainer in Asia, NA, Africa and Europe.

Gina's regional female leadership programs empower women to define, choose, navigate and find their unique leadership voice at home and on global corporate platforms. She is considered an expert on developing resilience, authentic impact, and presence with her unique CABI™ model (Confidence & Courage, Articulating with impact, Branding, Inquiry). Gina is the co-founder of three companies, including Catalyst Consulting HK.

She lives in Hong Kong with her husband and is a mother to a son and daughter.

You can connect with Gina at:

✉ : gina@catalysthk.com

in : https://www.linkedin.com/in/ginamaresciacatalyst/

STORY FIFTEEN

The Target is Just There Ahead of You, Stay Focused

When you face reality, you have already conquered all adversity.

I grew up a Caribbean Island girl and became a Global Citizen, an International Banker, a Financial Advisor, a Strategic Advisor to the government, and an Entrepreneur, CEO and Chairman of Swiss Financial Engineering, a company I co-founded after working for the UBS bank AG in Switzerland, I reached all of these targets despite facing major economic struggles during my childhood after my father passed away.

Therefore I strongly believe it's not where you come from; it's not the size of your past difficulties, but where you are heading is very important. We cannot change the past, but we can stir the present and take full control of our future. Perseverance is one of the golden keys to success.

Growing up on a paradise island, life is normally simple and smooth. I was just 10 years old when my Dad passed away. I was his princess, his heartstring and he was my whole world.

After my father's death, external factors took the family into crisis. Simple bureaucratic issues from the American pension fund that could have been avoided caused irrevocable harm, putting a complete household into economic difficulties.

I was the youngest of seven siblings. Despite the hardship we were going through, my mom was very focused on us. She was as hard as iron, strict as a General in the military and as independent as no other woman in the world. I will say I inherited this quality from her. She never stopped smiling and implementing her rules into our lives. We were always reminded of the importance of accomplishing my study to move to the next step. As we were obliged to respect our elder siblings, I have always looked up to my elder sister as a mother figure, as she sacrificed a lot to help my mother raise us.

But the main story is about how my mother overcomes the economic burden she faces a few months after my father's death and what it meant to my life back then. What did these hard experiences teach me?

First of all, my father passed, leaving me with a broken heart and a gap in my life forever. It was very hard on me. I experienced a collapsed world, as there was a special bond between us It was a day and night pain and tear. I thought I had to work on my trauma from his death, but suddenly, I realised my mom was not doing well. She became very busy and struggled to pay for all the outstanding bills and services after spending all her savings.

We had a settled life before as my fathers worked all his professional life for the US government and was enjoying his retirement on the island getting his pension. After he passed, my mom didn't get my father's pension she was entitled to for over three years. This took my family to a catastrophic economic crisis. My mom was in a deep pit of pain and sorrow and needed to find a way out so she and her seven kids could survive.

My mom was under a lot of pressure day and night from the American retirement officers or supervisors for no reason. But she kept her cool. She remained strong and focused, with only one target – to provide food and education for her seven children. She always said we couldn't give up. We will fight back against every challenge that comes in our direction. Although I knew she was suffering, she quietly taught us a major lesson about success and perseverance.

It hurt me to see my mom suffering, and I knew it also hurt my siblings. However, I was convinced we could all help my mother overcome the adversity, pain and sorrow she was facing. I approached my siblings, and we all started working our butts off with my mom, making food sales every Wednesday in the island's centre. It soon became very popular. Day by day and week by week, it showed progress, improvement, and commitment. My mom's food, made using my grandmother's recipes, became very popular.

Slowly but surely, we were all rewarded by demonstrating our ability to be successful in the face of adversity. We measured our successes and failures daily and committed ourselves to continuous learning and improvement. While helping my mom, as the youngest kid at home, I felt the need and obligation to support her. I saw her working around the clock. She was baking cakes and bread, cooking huge pots of stewed fish and other delicious island dishes. I always thought I must work harder no matter what I needed to lower her burdens and make her proud of me.

Therefore I asked her to allow me to work during my school holidays and needed a work permit as I was a minor. My mother hesitated and gave rules and conditions to my request because she knew I could practice my language skills therefore, she approved and gave me the approval letter. I then got my first job at a travel agency. I was assigned relationship manager as I was learning German to communicate with the guests in their language at the airport. I was proud to earn a very good salary plus tips while only 13 years old. My Mom was proud of me as well as I was able to support my mom. I focused on becoming the girl my father would have been proud of.

Learning various languages was like a golden key. **It opened so many doors and created links to amazing people giving wider and better access to new cultures and people.** I kept my focus on becoming a great professional to support my mother and the rest of my family. I kept my discipline in sports by playing tennis and going to the gym four to five times per week. I became a model and acted in films and tv soap operas but never lost touch with the reality that study was a priority in my path throughout my journey.

After a few years, I moved from the island to the mainland to finish my gymnasium and continue my university studies. I started studying and working. I was able to work and finance my education at one of the best private universities in the country. I have never attended a group or wild party during my study, except if it was organised by the university directly.

I earned my Bachelor's with Honours in International Trade and Economics and a Master's in Finance. After completing my studies, I moved to Germany to marry my husband and joined one of the major banks to start my career as a trainee.

I was learning intensively about international banking and the Wall Street movements. I was blessed to be given the great privilege of becoming a banker in a male-dominated world where only 5% of the employees in the German banking industry were women. After being selected, I committed myself to making it to the top.

Today as I reflect on my path, I share my success story of becoming an investment banker, working for the top banks in Germany, including UBS AG, where I managed approximately USD2,5 billion. I then moved to Switzerland to work for the UBS AG headquarters after being internally headhunted from the German branch. After working for a top bank in Germany, my transit into Switzerland was considered unconventional due to my cultural background.

I never thought of difficulties. Every woman in banking will face certain obstacles as it's a man's world, but without women and girls, nothing is possible. Therefore those obstacles that I faced from envy and malicious hearts have never bothered me. I think they even helped me to grow and to know the exact path I wanted to choose, to make it clear that I didn't want to work for a salary but for my passion.

However, I decided to thrive in moving forward, lifting my head to make the most of the unique opportunity given to me. After leading my third career in the banking industry, private banking and working with high-net-worth clients, I decided to assert my independence. I left the UBS bank to create my own asset management company and become an entrepreneur in finance.

Between my bank job and my position as CEO, Chairman and Co-founder of Swiss Financial Engineering AG, I have travelled 90% of the world. I have sat with several presidents and ministers and met with Kings and Sheiks. Today, due to all my effort, I live in the most iconic building in the world in Dubai. I support my charity with more than 7,500 children, giving back in return with love what God gave me in blessings.

My greatest advice to everyone is to be realistic in life. We can't change the past, but we can certainly manage our present for a better future. When you face reality, you have already conquered all adversity. Therefore, don't focus on where you are coming from, be focused on where you are heading.

We can only build the path and road for a better tomorrow when we know how we are standing today. I urge you to see through the obstacles and barriers you may face. Non-believers and roadblocks are not deterrents. Find ways to overcome difficulties, inspire and lead life to a brighter future.

When I remember my journey, my family crisis and my great and responsible mother, I am reminded of Winston Churchill's speech in 1942 during the Second World War. He stated:

"We shall go forward together. The road upwards is stony. There are upon our journey dark and dangerous valleys through which we have to make and fight our way. But it is sure and certain that if we persevere – and we shall persevere – we shall come through these dark and dangerous valleys into a sunlight broader and more genial and more lasting than mankind has ever known.

My final advice is to stay focused on the goal and not let obstacles deter you from finding the path forward. My journey was not the smoothest, but it's still brilliant. We must always be prepared to hold on to opportunities we come across. I will advise everyone to strive for education as it's one of the bases for success.

One of the most important life lessons that I have learned is the importance of patience. Patience is defined as an individual's ability to wait for something significant to happen without feeling frustrated due to the delay. In life, you'll have to wait for many things without feeling negative. If you could live by this lesson, your path will be bright and your future secure.

I hold persistence and discipline as a combined base for success. If you focus on your target and hold on to reaching your goals through investment in your personal development, you will always have the chance to be given opportunities up to the top.

Throughout my life, I have always thought I should never have an enemy, and I invite you to reflect on this. The friendlier your surroundings, the better your chances for professional development.

My key learnings:

- Focus on reaching your targets no matter your obstacles.
- Always prepare for the best to come, close old chapters and regenerate with a new vision.
- Prepare yourself to face life by investing in your education.

- Be patient as everything comes into your life at the right time for the right reason.
- Perseverance is key to your development. Never give up.
- Value the past, appreciate the present and prepare for a greater future.
- Be thankful for life and cherish with gratitude the support you receive from others.
- Share your success with your support team, and always seek a new path to grow.
- Be bold, be brave and face life's challenges to the end.
- Be loyal, faithful and sincere to people around you.

ABOUT THE AUTHOR

ANA LUCIA LIND

Ana Lucia Lind is an international banker, financial advisor, asset/wealth manager and investor. She is an entrepreneur and strategic advisor to Governments and devoted philanthropist.

She is recognised as a leading expert in finance in the emerging markets Asia, Africa, Latin America and the Middle East. She builds bridges between emerging markets and industrialised countries.

Anna Lucia has worked in leadership positions at the UBS Bank Head Quarter in Switzerland, UBS Bank Frankfurt-Germany, Julius Baer and Metzler Bank Frankfurt and at Swiss Capital Engineering AG Zurich before Co-founding Swiss Financial Engineering AG.

In her role as asset and fund manager for the UBS Bank Frankfurt, she has managed over US$2.5 billion. She started her career in investment banking in Germany and has been a guest speaker at various economic forums worldwide.

She devotes her life to more than seven thousand children throughout the world.

You can connect with Ana at:

✉ : analucia.lind@sfe-ag.com

in : https://www.linkedin.com/in/ana-lucia-lind-8b595517/

Instagram : https://www.instagram.com/analuciathe_1/

STORY SIXTEEN

To Be and Be Connected

Being together is not the same as being connected.

In an increasingly volatile world, what does "being connected" mean? Is it the point where the degrees of separation collapse? Or can we assuredly say it is an indicator of the robustness of our relationships?

Among the most cherished memories from my childhood are the spontaneous outdoor dinners with my maternal grandmother at her family home in Kerala. Against the backdrop of a very starry sky, *Amoomma* (grandmother) would gather us outside the family house, where my sister and I would sit cross-legged on large sheet-lined straw mats on the sand with our parents, aunts and all our cousins. Over endless helpings of curried tapioca and fish, washed down with jaggery-laced black coffee, listening to stories and neighbourhood news from the elders whilst catching up with my cousins. There was no place in the world I wanted to be than in their midst!

"Invisible threads are the strongest ties."

- Friedrich Nietzsche

From a very young age, I found myself happiest among people. Growing up in a convent boarding school during my initial school days in India amidst hundreds of kids from all backgrounds to completing my schooling in the Middle East alongside thousands of kids who spoke different languages, the commune has always been my comfort zone.

My parents loved entertaining and having people over at home; my recollections of most weekends growing up in

Doha are of family, friends, food, conversations and lots of laughter. They have played a huge part in moulding me into the "people connector" I am today. My sense of community, identity, belonging and attachment comes from them ensuring that my sister and I grew up amidst a community – that we grew up #connected. Having meals together, travelling in a group, watching movies and enjoying theatre together or just being with my people is the only way of life I knew growing up.

I remember resenting my parents for sending my sister and me to a boarding school and separating me from my mother when they moved to the Middle East with my father's new role. But the convent opened our world to a new way of life, a new religion, to find a family outside of our own, and allowed us to become independent, vocal and fearless young women. It was our true learning ground for community building, and to this day, my sister and I treasure our times there amid loving nuns, church bells and freshly baked bread!

Fast forward to my years in the Middle East – growing up, building a family in Doha, and building a career across the GCC – it was an effervescent and connected yet very protected environment. Surrounded always by family, friends and colleagues, one can get very comfortable in the safe space and the assurance it offers. Almost too comfortable, you expect every other place in the world to be as safe, assured, simple, and connected.

I felt miserable when my parents retired and moved back home to India. Suddenly the Middle East was not as enticing or simple, or connected for me anymore. My world had shrunk, and I did not enjoy being there anymore. A new job opportunity to move to Singapore was a welcome distraction offering the chance to rebuild and reconnect personally and professionally.

The relocation to Singapore was not without its share of challenges. Unlike the countries where I earlier lived and worked, I did not have any family in Singapore. I had a group of friends in Singapore from my business school, and they were the main reason I considered moving to a new country, culture and lifestyle. The first few years of settling in were interesting, to put it mildly. The work culture was new. A distinct lack of belonging in the workplace and a "local-foreigner divide" was all too new for me. I had never experienced a "them and us" differentiation during my 12 years working in the Middle East. Having my batch mates to lean on was a huge blessing while figuring out my space in Singapore.

The move did not bode well for my marriage or my health, and it eventually took its toll. In those three years, my ex-husband and I decided to part ways. I struggled to embrace the role of a single parent with two young kids to care for whilst working a full-time job that involved regular travel, nursing multiple slipped discs in my back and being diagnosed with hypothyroidism. I missed my parents and my extended support system, and the comfort of a familiar environment.

Walking alone was not a journey I was used to or enjoyed

doing. It was an unfamiliar and uncomfortable territory that drained my energy endlessly. There were many occasions when I couldn't find a decent house for rent because of my nationality, but now being a single mother was another disqualification for finding a home. The exclusion and isolation were sometimes extreme and made me wonder why I was still living in an unwelcome land, far from my own.

I would be lying if I said I did not consider moving back home or sending the kids to a boarding school back home where they are safe and can build communities of their own. I enjoyed my work and the growth that came with it. I also did not want to be separated from my kids or miss any opportunity to see them grow. I remember my resentment for being sent away to a boarding school although it made me a tougher girl, the resentment was real. I did not want to uproot my kids from the community and friendships they were beginning to build in Singapore, and I definitely did not want them to go through the same resentment. The divorce was enough of a blow to them at such a young age, and any relocation to a new, unfamiliar environment would not have helped them in any way then.

So, I decided to give blooming, where I was planted, a go.

They say when life throws you curveballs, you own those curves. I had no formula or experience in navigating these unfriendly waters. Still, the prospect of having a stable environment for my kids to grow up and learn and my somewhat selfish determination to make this work against all odds got me going. Despite the seemingly unfriendly exterior,

Singapore has offered me a different type of safe space where I could focus on my kids and my career and do it with the least interference. **Living here grounded me and made me readier than ever to face any more curveballs that dear life would throw my way.**

You can take Binu out of the community, but you can't take the community out of Binu, thankfully! Slowly and surely, I built my own tribe here in Singapore. Some of them are parents of my kids' friends, and some are folks I met while volunteering at work. And some of them are just people with similar mindsets, interests, and vibes; they hold space for me and are happy to run wild with me. I am proud to have found a beautiful bunch of such humans who simply support, nurture and enable me. **I would not have found this tribe if not for Singapore, so I am extremely grateful.**

In 2019, I found myself at a career crossroads. I had been in the retail industry in senior leadership roles for almost 20 years and was looking for my next challenge. Retail as an industry was declining; brands were downsizing their brick-and-mortar blueprint and expanding their online presence.

The growth opportunities were pretty much stagnant. As with many other industries, retail has a lot of work yet to be done, especially in building genuinely inclusive and equitable workplaces with belonging at their core. The signs were all there – it was time to move on and explore a new path: one that lets me do what I love doing the most, one that allows me to bring people together.

Active volunteering opened up a whole new world for me and is the foundation on which I have built my commune here in Singapore. It brought me into contact with a brilliant group of women and men who nurtured and nourished me when the chips were down. It is not about the number of people you know but the depth and realness of the relationships you build and grow, the depth of your connections, and about being grateful by valuing these amazing interactions and sharing lived experiences. That is the life lesson I take away from my volunteering experience for the past four years.

And over the last 18 months of the pandemic, we all experienced physical and emotional disconnection while we nurtured hopes to "get back to what it was before". **But we also learnt that being together is not the same as being connected.** This period also introduced me to a connection of a different kind – the connection with myself. I found joy in watching a movie alone, having a meal alone, or just spending time with myself – things I believed I was incapable of doing pre-pandemic. And I now simply enjoy shopping alone; it is the joy of a totally different dimension to shop without opinions and judgement, to buy something or just simply window shop. The biggest lesson from this period was that it is all about the experience and how people and things make you emotionally engage and feel.

And so, customer experience is an area that I am passionately invested in contributing, both from my past life as a retailer and as someone who strongly believes in creating holistic experiences for people and the wider community. Creating extraordinary and memorable experiences that transform into long-term relationships underpinned by human connection is the future of any sustainable business, in my opinion.

I started my business of connecting people during this period and discovered true joy in what it means to be humans together. My volunteering network gave me the conviction and courage to start independently and follow my passion. My life comes full circle #beingconnected. People, experiences and places connect the dots to who I am today; people being the most significant common factor and rightly so!

My organisation, B.Connected, is an embodiment of all that I am. I am thankful every day that I don't have to go to work. Instead, I get to do what I love the most: connecting people and being connected. As friends, partners, mentors or colleagues, the people that crossed my path or the ones that I brought together have shaped my journey this far.

There are many individuals and places who particularly made this journey possible – the ones who enabled and empowered me, the women and men who sent that lift down for me to step into my own. And I am extremely grateful for each one of them.

And so full circle it is – replete with the circle of friends within the circle of life and the opportunity to advance the human experience!

To truly connect with others, we must first be connected with ourselves. For everyone looking to understand what it means to be connected or to simply be, I would say:

- **Connectedness is not an end in itself.** It is the relationship and how it helps you to grow and to give that really matters.
- **Connect with depth, authenticity and consistency.** The most rewarding part of being connected is how it enables you to grow and evolve and how you can pay that forward.
- **Take time to disconnect intentionally.** Whether it is people or things, if it does not help you grow, evolve or contribute as a person, it is not worth your energy or time.

The invisible threads bind our communities and form our strong ties in our social connections and the community we create.

ABOUT THE AUTHOR

BINU BALAN

Binu Balan is a business expansion champion and business strategist with over 20 years of experience helping individuals and global brands create lasting brand equity.

Through her organisation B.Connected Pte Ltd, a B2B business matchmaking consultancy, she drives business partnering and stakeholder management with a unique service offering that combines market intelligence, business model diagnostics and access to a local and global network of service providers. She is passionate about customer experience and is an avid people connector, ignited by two decades of leading international operations for global fashion brands across the Middle East and APAC.

Binu volunteers full-time at KeyNote Women Speakers Directory, leading Speaker Placement, Business Development & Partnerships globally for the 300+ speakers in the directory and its partners.

Born in India and bred in the Middle East, Binu now calls Singapore home, living here with her two daughters. She holds an MBA in Marketing & International Business and is also a trained yoga practitioner and classical dancer.

You can connect with Binu at:

: binubb@outlook.com

: https://www.linkedin.com/in/binubalan/

STORY SEVENTEEN

Trust Your Gut Instinct!

I had a constant feeling of uneasiness

It was great to be back in London, my favourite city. I have travelled here regularly in the last 10 years and have always enjoyed all the seasons. Having been born and raised in Asia I struggled initially but my liking for the city grew every time I went back for a short holiday.

Now I had been relocated for a year to set up a family office. I was excited to stay and spend more time in London and started building my castle in the clouds.

A Senior Manager I was acquainted with in the Singapore office recommended me for the role. Our interaction was limited and cordial. When he asked if I would be open to moving to London as he was setting up the office there, I said yes and didn't think too much of it.

It was an excellent opportunity for me until that unfortunate morning. Days before the incident, I had a constant feeling of uneasiness. His way of communication has become more personal. He invited me out for dinner, but I had a prior engagement and hence politely declined. When I shared this feeling of unease with a friend, I was told I was overthinking it. I was still doubtful but ignored it, thinking it was my own imagination.

I had a trip to the US the following day and some official documents that I needed to bring along with me. My colleague, the senior manager, had to pass me a document before I left for the airport. It was 9 am and I was staying in a boutique hotel in Central London while sorting out an apartment. He came by the hotel reception and was directed to my room.

As I opened the door, he stepped in, handing the document to me. I took it from him and he placed his hands on my arms, saying, "Have a safe flight." I thanked him, and he moves in closer for a hug. Confused, I take a step back saying I will be leaving for the airport shortly. He continues by saying he's been trying to see me, but I have been busy while I was trying to clear up my desk.

He then caresses my arm and I look at him, asking what he is doing. He simply said, "It's ok," and comes in for another hug. I feel myself go stiff at this point and he tries to kiss my lips and I keep moving my face away. I feel his hands caressing my body; at this point, I say whatever he is doing is weird and wrong.

He keeps saying, "It's ok!" He continues trying to kiss me, and touch my face. I forcefully take a step back and sit back on the chair.

Completely solemn and silent. What just happened? I was confused. I sat in silence unable to lift my gaze, simply staring at my phone.

I was in a deep state of shock, while he sat in front of me across the edge of the bed, still smiling and asking what I am busy with on my phone when he is right there and that I should join him. My mind was a fog, I could not think, but with a shaky voice, I abruptly said that I would have to leave soon. He looked at me, quickly stood up, and said not to take offence to anything. It was just for fun!

I shut the door in his face, and there was a sudden outburst of uncontrollable tears. It was the realisation of what had just transpired, an invasion of my personal space and privacy, leaving me vulnerable. I spoke to a friend over the phone, and while he was trying his best to console me, it did not work.

However, he told me to call the predator and rebuke him for what he did, but I was hesitant to speak to him. Minutes later, I left a message to my predator and said he had done wrong and should not have touched me and misbehaved. He had invaded my privacy, and I was very affected now. I continued crying while getting ready to leave for the airport.

Fifteen minutes later, there was a knock on my door. I opened it and saw the predator was back while I was still on the phone speaking to my friend, tears rolling down my face like a waterfall. I could feel my face go pale as if I had just seen a ghost! I panicked as he moved into the room.

I told him to leave, but he kept saying it was an accident and didn't mean to misbehave. The call to my friend was still active, and just before he arrived, I took a screenshot of the message I sent him and sent it to my email. He asked me not to mention it to our boss and kept saying he would take care of me.

I was angered at this point and asked him what made him think it was ok to touch me without my permission. I was trembling as my anger rose, and I kept scolding him. I kept telling him to leave, but he started to show his fake tears of grief, a hypocrite at best.

Finally, he asked me to delete the message I had sent him! I refused to do it, and he continued with his crocodile tears. I was still traumatised and couldn't bear the sight of him, so I agreed to delete the message. He left, and I collapsed as I shut the door on him for the second time. I picked up my phone, and my friend couldn't say anything. He was in shock at what he had heard transpire.

In 40 minutes, I had gone through several emotions and was sobbing relentlessly on my way to the airport. I was unsure how I would make this long trip in this disturbed state. I had left a voice message for my best friend, who luckily lived less than an hour away from London. She called me back and said she was making her way down to me and that it would take her 40 minutes. I told her I had to take the flight out, and she said I shouldn't take the flight but should tell work what had happened.

As I sat waiting for her in the airport, I looked at my phone and dialled the wife of my boss, with whom I worked closely. I tried to keep myself together as I spoke to her, but I couldn't. I could barely complete my sentences. She figured something had happened and patiently waited for me to talk as I tried to calm myself down. I told her who misbehaved and that I would get in touch the next day and share further. I met my friend and stayed with her all week, not wanting to return to London.

During all this, the predator was constantly trying to reach me, but I was not responding to anyone's calls. I was in a safe place and was relieved to have someone I could reach out to. As I spoke to the wife the next day and described the incident, she was in shock and could not believe what he did as he was an extremely religious person in their eyes. I said I couldn't pretend and would leave the company if it took no action.

She said she understood my situation, but my boss may not. Welcome to the patriarchal society! I was ready to leave after hearing that I had nothing else to say. My boss called a few hours later and scolded me for not calling him immediately. He asked, "Are you sure? Were you drunk? He's the biggest scoundrel. I can't believe he did it!"

Those were his words. He said I don't have to worry. The predator would be taken care of, and I should return to London and confidently do my work. I was asked to call the senior manager, record the conversation about him accepting what he did, and send it over to my boss. I did as I was asked, and after hearing all this, he confessed and apologised, and I sent the recording to them. They listened, were shocked, and I was told not to share it with anyone. Fast forward to the present, the predator still works with them as he brings in the money, and it is considered not that big a deal.

Why did I not report the incident to the police? I had evidence. I could have instantly pushed him away. Why did I meet him in the hotel to hand over the documents? Why did I continue working for them? Does that make me weak?

All I can say is not everyone thinks or reacts in the same way. While it is easy to respond and instantly suggest when listening to such incidents, being in that moment is a whole different thing. My entire being just froze. While it took me a few minutes to react, my reaction was confused. It could have been worse, and I am thankful that nothing more happened, but it is a chilling experience.

Before this, I had only ever heard of situations like these, read of them, but never thought I'd be one of them. I was so engulfed in shock that it shook my intellectual understanding of right and wrong and dos and don'ts. I remember two friends telling me to "Get over it".

It is sad, but unfortunately, people still don't understand what it actually means when your privacy is invaded. It was a few months of struggle coming to terms with the incident, but the sound advice from an old friend was to seek therapy; otherwise, it would affect my future relationships. I could see it happening, I was very apprehensive of any male coming close to me, and I shut off from meeting male friends or acquaintances alone.

I went for a few months of therapy to overcome the trauma and work through my emotions; it was the best thing I did for myself. I know that I was not guilty nor at fault for being welcoming. What the predator thought of me was entirely on him. How people perceive me honestly has nothing to do with me, but it is their business. My business is to take care of my emotional needs and how I feel about myself.

While I forgave him for what he did, I still can't condone his behaviour. I forgive, so I no longer need to hold on to the past. While I was grateful for the support I had from my sister and friends, I still had to work with myself on overcoming the experience, and it was not a very pleasant journey diving in.

In any journey or difficulty, it is never easy, but only you can make it work in your favour. You either cry over it all your life, or you deal with it and become stronger. Don't ever shut yourself out because many will stand for you. My heart goes out to all the women who experience these deeply traumatising behaviours of men.

While I know some men have immense respect for women and empower them without any judgement or favours in return, we are still a long way to changing the societal norms, but it is progressing. The biggest takeaway for me, trust my gut! I felt it and ignored it. It has the innate wisdom to tell you what you don't know. Always trust it.

ABOUT THE AUTHOR

SADHNA UPADHYA

Sadhna Upadhya is a Yogi based in London, United Kingdom, with 2500 hours of teaching experience. She comes from a professional background in hospitality and management with 15 years of experience.

Born and bred in Singapore, she has travelled extensively in the last few years pursuing her passion for teaching and has amplified this by a wanderlust of exploring European cities simultaneously. Her portfolio includes working with many luxury hotel brands such as the Far East Hospitality Group, Four Seasons, Ritz Carlton and many other corporate organisations providing yoga training services.

She is actively engaged in bringing her own wellness app, "Shunya", to life, which will be launched in the latter part of the year. Her purpose is to give back to the community through yoga. Sadhna firmly believes that one's quality of life is determined through daily habits with discipline in place.

You can connect with Sadhna at:

✉ : sadhna01@hotmail.com

in : https://www.linkedin.com/in/sadhna-upadhya-54a4941a/

🌐 : www.shunyaapp.com

STORY EIGHTEEN

Whatever Happens, Happens For The Good

I am surprised at how much I have grown.

We scrambled to catch our train as we saw it leaving the station. "Whatever happens, happens for the good," my Nana (maternal grandfather) said. This is also written in the holy Hindu book of Bhagawad Gita, and I have come to believe in this strongly. At that moment, however, I wondered aloud what good could come from missing our train!

We got a call from a close family member who had faced a health crisis. Had we been on that train, we wouldn't have been able to help in time. We were exactly where we needed to be. This was my first tryst with "whatever happens, happens for the good". So here I am sharing my life story as I rummage through different anecdotes that make me who I am, with this mantra at the heart of it.

Childhood experiences

I grew up in Mumbai, India and had a magical and secure childhood filled with family holidays, hobbies, and close friends. My early experiences include travelling the world with my parents and brother, honest and invigorating dinner table discussions, disagreeing and yet supporting each other through different situations. Along with academics, my parents also focused on raising us to be kind, compassionate and humble humans. This shaped me as a person, secure in my skin, strong and fiercely protective of the ones I love.

Although I was a good kid in school, competitive examinations were not my forte. In Class X, I performed abysmally in my preliminary examinations before the final Boards. My worst performance was in the English Language. My then English teacher very bluntly said to my mother, "This is an indicator of what she will get eventually – do not expect any magic". This was not something you wanted to hear at the tender age of fifteen when you were trying to prove yourself.

I am glad my parents motivated me to look beyond this and instilled in me the confidence that I could excel – this became the turning point that propelled my performance. I got Grade A (90 out of 100) in my final Class X Board Exams in English and a stellar performance overall. It was sheer hard work, perseverance, positivity and support from my constant cheerleaders – my parents and my brother.

My school motto was "There is no excellence without labour". This became my life mantra as well. I achieved my goals and paved the way for myself but none through chance or luck. I am happy that life shaped up this way and grateful that I have strived to achieve every milestone. When success comes with hard work, one treasures it that much more. When life throws curveballs, it is hard – but when you look back, you realise how pieces of the jigsaw come together to make sense.

Quarter-life explorations

After completing my MBA in the UK, I was keen to work for a couple of years before I moved back to my home in Mumbai. However, life had other plans. If someone had told me when I was leaving London that I would advise a C-level audience to become a respected thought leader in my field, and this journey would begin with my corporate life in Mumbai – I would not have believed my ears.

I got to share my view on the telecom industry in Asia through my press quotes in television and newspapers. This pushed me out of my comfort zone as I was a shy kid in school. I was putting myself out there, making connections and networking while sharing my strategic advice and expert comments on the trending topics in technology.

Back then, I was sure that Mumbai was where I wanted to be – my family, my career, my dreams – this was the place for me. I soon met and got engaged to someone who also saw his future in Mumbai. However, life is what happens to you when you are busy making other plans.

That engagement did not work out, and soon I got laid off from my job due to restructuring. I was 27 years old – unemployed, and single. It was not easy for someone with a broken engagement to be a "socially acceptable" match in India around 2010. My self-confidence hit an all-time low.

It was during this time that I met my now husband. I was convinced this would be a one-time meeting when I met him. Not because he was not interesting, but because I went with preconceived notions about boys who grew up in South Mumbai (it turns out I had met all the pretentious ones before him). Also, he told me that he might relocate to Southeast Asia someday. These things did not fit in my head as I saw my future in Mumbai. But here I am, married to this wonderful man for a decade now, living a happy life in Singapore. Did I say, "whatever happens, happens for the good?"

Married life and career struggles

I married into a big family, a change coming from a small nuclear family. I manoeuvred through building relationships with my husband's parents, elder sisters and their families across borders and ages while understanding the nuances of human relationships.

When I reached Singapore, it was a home away from home. I found it very easy to settle in and was amazed to see how much it had to offer in terms of culture, cuisines, outdoor parks, nature trails and activities to do as a couple or as parents of young kids. After nine years of living in Singapore, I still discover new things about the city.

My husband and I bonded over our love for travel. We travelled extensively in the region, exploring spectacular locations with unique cultures. We met interesting people from different walks of life and tried local cuisines while building memories.

I did not land a job in Singapore immediately upon arriving. Instead, I got a job in Johor Bahru, Malaysia. While being a dependent in Singapore, I was on a work visa in Malaysia. Back then, it felt like a trek – three days a week going across the border to another country to work, getting my passport stamped through immigration over a hundred times and heading back the same evening to Singapore. I was floating on two boats and felt conflicted and unsettled, and I questioned myself several times.

It all paid off a year later when I found a full-time position in Singapore – incidentally, my Malaysian job was the one that was the stepping stone for the Singapore job. This has been the pattern of all my career moves so far. My learnings and skills from previous jobs have always helped me land my next job – it is all connected.

Building a family

I was working as a tech industry expert and getting invited for panel discussions and speaking engagements to share my insights as a woman in technology. I also spearheaded the research program for the internet of things and urban ecosystems in the Asia Pacific region.

Around this time, we were also trying to expand our family. Like a lot of modern couples, we had difficulties in conceiving. My incredible boss understood these struggles and gave me time and flexibility to manage this journey and work.

The fertility journey was life-altering – there was much left to chance, science, and God's will. I put my body through hundreds of hormone injections, and we poured in lots of prayers and money to make this happen. The first time did not work out, and it came as a blow. It made me feel inadequate and broken. I felt that my body had failed me. Emotionally it was a dark phase, and while my family was supportive – it was a lonely journey with no promise of a positive outcome.

With the doctor's guidance, we went in for our second cycle almost immediately after the first failed. And it worked. When I went for my first ultrasound to confirm the pregnancy, the doctor detected not one but two heartbeats. After almost six years of having no kids, we were showered with two blessings. My twins were born prematurely and spent three weeks in the NICU.

Although we had the best medical care, it was hard to see them tiny, helpless, and away from us. Premature babies are always harder to look after due to low immunity and delayed milestones. God had given us two little fighters. They eventually got off their breathing support and other infections and came home to us – our arms and hearts were full.

Motherhood was perhaps always on the cards, but the journey there was unique. It made me realise that sometimes situations are beyond our control. I also learnt to process failures better while harbouring the hope that it will work out in the end. When I look at my little boy and girl – I feel they are living examples of "whatever happens, happens for the good".

Exhilarating motherhood while finding balance

The arrival of babies brought about a big change in our lives. A baby in your life can turn everything upside down. From breastfeeding to managing schedules to alternating between their needs to the simplest tasks can sometimes become a project.

During COVID-19, I was engulfed in baby duties while trying to work from home after my maternity leave. That is when I was let go from my role due to my company's restructuring. However, since they valued my contribution, I moved to a contractual position with the same company in the interim.

That is when I met a woman technology leader who took an interest in my profile and brought me on board my current organisation. She looked beyond challenges such as economic headwinds, hiring freezes and early motherhood to employ me. A big part of my career growth has been possible due to such supportive leaders and mentors, for which I am eternally grateful.

Twin toddler shenanigans

Motherhood has taught me a lesson in multi-tasking, planning and patience. It has taught me life hacks that I never thought I needed. I am surprised at how much I have grown.

While my husband has been supportive, as a young working mother of twin toddlers, I constantly find myself in situations that challenge me. Sometimes both kids want you at once, and they know how to gang up and throw tantrums to push your limits. I must have felt like cloning myself multiple times over the last couple of years.

In January 2022, amidst the third COVID wave, I travelled alone with 2.5-year-old toddlers and an insane amount of luggage from India to Singapore. Due to travel restrictions, neither my husband nor my mum could travel with me. I survived – with lots of anxious moments, nevertheless. After this, I never got worried about taking care of them alone – it changed me in a good way.

Whenever I get nervous, I realise that God only gives us as much as he thinks we can handle. I was meant to be a mother of twins. I was meant to make this work. I was meant to wait to get here when I could balance my personal and professional front. It all happened in its own time.

Parting thoughts

I believe each life experience has led me to the next and formed a coherent story in my life. I strongly believe in hard work and prayers. My thinking has evolved, and I try not to get daunted by challenges. I have become patient, resilient, flexible, open to change and better at handling my emotions in overwhelming situations. I am still a work in progress. Each day I try to be a better version of myself. Unusual people do not do different things; they do things differently. I feel the same about myself and my journey.

ABOUT THE AUTHOR

SHAILY SHAH

Shaily Shah is a technology expert working across research and consulting profiles with prominent multinationals such as E&Y, Citibank, Gartner, IDC and others over the past 14 years. Since moving to Singapore eight years ago, she has focused on driving technology research across the Asia Pacific region. She has expertise in trailblazing market trends such as telecom, IoT (Internet of Things), smart cities and cloud computing, for which she has authored crisp whitepapers and research reports.

She has been invited to speak at and participated in and moderated industry panel discussions at conferences and summits for corporate and government clients. She has also provided succinct bytes and press quotes as an industry expert on India and Southeast Asia's key developments and market landscape trends.

Outside work, she is fond of creative writing, watching plays, meeting new people, exploring different cuisines, and travelling worldwide while building innumerable memories with her family. She is a young working mother who enjoys parenting her twins with her husband.

You can connect with Shaily at:

✉ : shaily.a.shah@gmail.com

in : https://www.linkedin.com/in/shailyshah/

STORY NINETEEN

Which of My Roles Takes Priority?

A small pause to attend Life took me a few additional years and adjustments to be back on track as I had dreamt!

The Present

Currently, I am living and experiencing life differently from what I had ever imagined it to be. My decision to have a full-blown career outside the home, in other words, two full-time jobs, has made life exceptionally complicated. I don't wish to choose one over the other, I can't ever separate myself from either. I chose to give up active engagement in a few other roles. I know things will change when my kids move out of the home. The cliché for me is to say, I put family above my career. Honestly, I often struggle with this idea, how could I put the well-being of my kids above or below the well-being of my career or vice versa?

As a clinician, I have been trained to believe that if I feel satisfied as an individual, I would be a happy mum, colleague, employer, wife, daughter, or friend. Whilst having worked for thousands of hours over the last 14 years helping clients unpack their lives, I have realized that my work is core to my existence or one can say my identity. The question is not whether it's right or wrong, it is who I really am. I am not ashamed to say this, if I do have someone to blame, it's me. I always visualized myself as a working professional.

The craziness of where I am in my life started in early 2016. Overnight from being a freelancer therapist, I became an owner and clinical lead of 43-year-old mental health practice. It was a legacy that I took over, it was a wild dream come true. I was excited, but also fearful of failure. By this time my life's motto ' never give up' was in play. The urge to quit was very high. I was at peak of my professional and personal growth

The next 3-4 years meant all work no play at home and in the office. The company was in shambles and needed a complete makeover. Life was tough, both kids and the company needed me. Soon after the takeover, I was grieving my older child leaving for college. Always worst when the first child leaves home. Responsibilities don't reduce they multiply as kids grew with age. The question was how will I cope with increasing demands. Quitting was very tempting. A few days were harder than the others. Looks like I was out to conquer the world with some kind of revenge.

When COVID-19 hit, my sixth sense suggested an unprecedented time. Soon we were in lockdown. As a leader, I was responsible for ensuring support to everyone, whether it was a client or a staff. The challenges were because of no guidelines or precursors, I had to lead to ensure safety and support. Simultaneously, I also needed to ensure my family and kids were safe. The everyday threat of contracting the virus at work and bringing it to my kids was real. We all worked overtime for three years without any breaks, quitting wasn't a choice even then. During this time, I went to India to attend to my father's medical issues. At the first peak of Covid-19, with every passing moment, I feared for his and my life. It felt like I was just a few inches from death. It frazzles me how he and I escaped untethered. These five days changed how I see life, returned home full of gratitude for my life.

Transition to private practice and why?

The writing was on the wall, and inflexibility at work was preventing me from being able to balance home and work. The 3 kids, who needed me. I had to find a way to do both. I was mindful my second chance came after 10 years and by now I had invested 3 years into the new career. My stakes were high and options limited something different had to be done to keep both going.

With every passing moment, my fears hijacked every waking moment. I didn't know where to start. I didn't know many people in this profession. This profession wasn't discussed in my social circles in fact was looked down upon. The fear of just being a stay home mum motivated me to spend a few weeks exploring options. It was the same time Google's search engine came into play. Many sleepless nights led me to a multidisciplinary clinic that accepted me.

The journey was tougher than I ever imagined. I sat idle for a year. A big believer in the power of the universe, most colleagues at the practice came to rescue. For a year I did everything that others didn't want to do to get visibility. Both work and home were in full force. Being an involved parent to three kids was a tough job. My fight was against my own situation, my goals were clear and I was in no rush. Life had taught me to keep going, the pace didn't matter.

My life to an outsider was of a full-time mum attending school events, organizing playdates, doing bedtimes, organizing birthday parties, and doing college applications. On the inside, it meant three to four hours of sleep every week. My challenges were mine, I was setting up my private practice. My interests, priorities, and lifestyle changed. I was no longer that same stay home mum or wife. Additionally, this meant I no longer had the luxury of doing things unintentionally. I was creating something for myself, and the cost was a lack of freedom of time.

Interestingly, family and friends couldn't understand what I was doing and why was I doing? On the contrary, everyone felt, I had everything, a supportive husband & family, financial security, and a fancy lifestyle. At times, my presence made people uncomfortable. I noticed confusion and questions, rejections and abandonment from others.

By this time, I had an identity. I was mentioned on social media, as word of mouth was spreading. This eventually led to me starting another practice at a different location.

Finally I felt at peace with myself. The internal conflict had vanished. My own identity was something I craved in the last 13 years when circumstances led me to give up my job overnight.

Upon reflection, I wasn't able to address others' confusion, as I didn't have the answers myself. Looking back, if I took a pause to reflect I wouldn't be where I am now. Slowing down, was not an option I gave myself. It took a lot to come this far. The second time around, I had more experience with life, more determined and intentional with my goals.

By then, I had more clarity, that I needed something more than just being a wife and mother to feel fulfilled. It was high time I created something for myself, with a purpose, an identity, something to cherish and own.

Getting into this profession

There came a time in our lives when one of us had to give up careers to keep the family together whilst there was growth for the other partner. As an individual, it was never just about me but was about everyone involved. I wouldn't have been happy if my husband had given up his career for me. In our case the choice was obvious, his job came with perks, and provided financial stability, and a good lifestyle. By this time, I had given his career and my son ten years.

My work helped me understand how the pent-up feelings presented themselves. Only a trained eye could have caught it, but unfortunately, no one knew I was struggling internally. It is clear that the absence of my own identity and financial independence was creating internal havoc.

I had always been fortunate in terms of financial stability, firstly provided by my parents and then by my husband. The mere thought of not having financial independence was another internal struggle. With many years of soul-searching and introspection, I believe that financial independence meant freedom. Again that's who I am. I now, know that freedom is the core of my identity. It's a part of me that I can't control or change. I also know that when my freedom is compromised, it throws me off the curve, and I react badly. I often see similar traits and struggles in my clients, the presentation may be different but underlying issues may be similar.

At 13 I made the most significant decision of my life to move to India to attend high school away from my parents. The move was a shock to my existence, trauma is the word in psychology, and was against my parent's wishes. I suffered from low-grade fever for an entire year; no doctors could make any diagnosis. It was more psychological rather than physical, but again quitting was not an option. My understanding was that a high-quality education will be the key to a flourishing career later on. Though I barely saw my family yet it was about me succeeding in whatever I do, and giving up was never a choice I gave myself.

Though I often blamed relocation (because of my husband's job) as a reason for me not having a career, I also had ethical issues delegating my children's care to others. The best option would be to outsource parenting to a nanny while I was at work. With the birth of the twins the internal conflict got stronger and stronger, I sensed it would be detrimental to my well-being, and unhealthy for the family. I needed a purpose bigger than just being a mother and wife. I have no real memory of why I decided to study psychology except that I could come to attend classes irrespective of the country I lived in.

As per Asian standards, it was pretty late in life to go back to school. Once again, I put myself in an unusually difficult situation where fear, doubt, and insecurity all hit me at once. I struggled considerably being a mum of three kids and doing a Master's level degree course. Quitting is not a choice I ever opted for.

What the Future Holds..

I am moving into the future filled with mixed feelings. I am curious about what the future may hold, with the company's acquisition in progress. It's a milestone that any entrepreneur would have dreamt of. As I go through it, I am mindful, of what's next. I am repeatedly exploring, what more can I do or what I want to achieve. What next, will fulfill me?

These days I notice opportunities everywhere. It seems that the universe has opened itself up, but the next steps will need some introspection, and reflection as a professional, as a mother, and in the other roles I play. Like anyone else I have high ambitions, but my kids need me as much as I need my aspirations to be fulfilled. I do want to fulfill the responsibilities of all my roles, it's never going to be one at the cost of the other. With this, I am again choosing a path that will be full of challenges.

My advice to readers

My journey has been long and challenging, with some failures and successes. Most experiences have taught me valuable life lessons. One of the biggest lesson life has taught me has to not give up no matter how hard things get. With time things and situations change for the better. In times of challenges, the pace doesn't matter, what matters most was to keep moving ahead toward the goals.

Life is about fulfilling different roles; for me, it's never about choosing one over the other. I intend to fulfill all my roles to the best of my ability. Life, for me, has to be about purpose. It's about taking a step forward daily in my purpose and, in other words, leading a life with a growth mindset and intentions. With these goals, I hope I make a great role model for my kids and others around me.

ABOUT THE AUTHOR

VINTI MITTAL

Vinti Mittal is the Clinical Director at SACAC Counselling and a registered counsellor and clinical member of the Singapore Association of Counselling with 15 years of experience.

In her current role, she is heavily invested in the well-being of her clients and the practice's clients. She spends considerable time consulting with her clients and providing staff supervision. Vinti also offers clinical supervision to other upcoming therapists in the field.

Vinti is passionate about the roles of physical health and lifestyle in an individual's well-being. She sees herself as a restless soul in the gym, walking in nature or out in her free time. She sees life differently after being trained as a counsellor.

She is a very involved mother of three boys. She learns a lot from life, her kids, and her clients.

You can connect with Vinti at:

✉ : vintimittal2019@gmail.com

in : https://www.linkedin.com/in/vinti-mittal-43a1307/

STORY TWENTY

Zone. Brace. Engage. UP.

Find your calling. Feed it. And lift.

I am an island girl. Born and raised in a matrilineal family. We are taught to believe that daughters inherited the earth. A tad bit contrarian to the rest of the world, as you can imagine. A fascinating way of life. It was the only one I knew. Born into a family of dancers, we were polyglots – the lot of us. Dance was yet another language we learnt, cultivated, cherished and passed on to the next generation.

Dance – movement, discipline, structure. It was our language to hold and nurture. It was our language of love. Training, rehearsals, practice sessions, conditioning routines – that was just our way of life since I was four years old – "stand tall, back straight, slouch for a pouch" were all missives, I recall, vividly, in early childhood. School life was replete with dance medals, trophies, and competitions far and wide. My agility came in handy for all track and field contests. School champions, state champions, inter-collegiate festival champions – the list went on.

Training, rehearsals, conditioning, teamwork and flawless stage performances and impromptu saves – extremely essential life skills, as I was about to discover. But back then, it was all about glorious wins, championships and celebrating well-earned victories. Proud moments. Moments of joy, exhilaration, and celebration. Wins. Joy all around. Strategy, choreography, and execution – critical to the win.

We drove far and wide to see diverse performances, watch different dance forms, appreciate the choreography and just live the vibe. But also, most importantly, to learn from the best, build on it and create my distinct style. I was the principal dancer by the time I was 18. I trained my own troupe and choreographed and delivered several public performances.

And then, just like that, the inevitable happened. I moved on. I moved cities, colleges, countries, and jobs. And suddenly I was looking at myself as someone who hadn't delivered a stage performance in over two decades. I was that person I didn't think I would be when I was a grown up. I had always imagined myself dancing on stage, as a child.

Having lived and worked in four different geographies, managed multicultural, high-performing teams, a long-distance marriage (in some parts) and raised a child in three of these, the magnitude of my gift and how I had let it slide suddenly dawned on me, during the pandemic.

Somewhere, I felt the need to anchor myself in a new discipline. I was beginning to miss the camaraderie of training buddies, the early morning call times, and the allure of the prep before stage time.

I found a running buddy. But it wasn't for long. We had moved countries again. I needed my serotonins. I was introduced to trampoline jumping. High adrenaline and serious skill. So captivating. But keeping up with 14-year-olds, however fascinating, is a bit daunting. And then, just like that, I found my new island of endorphins.

Lifting. I am very aware that this could sound terribly misleading.

Powerlifting, to be clear.

It wasn't immediate or instant.

The first time I was introduced to a barbell, it felt cold and alien. Neither of us willing to budge an inch. I was in…hook, line and sinker.

The time I spent trying to lift iron was directly proportional to how resolute I became in wanting to be strong enough to do so. Come to think of it lifting is a lot like dancing. Every single element needs to work in perfect harmony for the lift to be flawless and injury-free.

My years of training and discipline kicked in. I was relentless. I would constantly read in a bid to acquire knowledge. Form, nutrition, technique. On loop.

I wanted to absorb everything. I would stare shamelessly, at all the lifters, to try and emulate, from those who had spent years in perfecting it to an art form. I had to let go of what I thought was the ideal body type. I had to unlearn a gazillion things to be able to make space for the new.

I had to build my neural pathways to be able to lift. I didn't miss sessions. I would be up at 5 am to train to create enough time for everything else, including the office, schoolwork and kitchen duties. No excuses. No regrets. I aimed to lift 100 kilos (220 pounds) someday.

I think it might be important to set the context, critical even.

I could barely lift 50 kilos (110 pounds) which was about 90% of my body weight.

The barbell is 20 kilos (Olympic barbell), and one set of plates took it to 50. I would be grunting and grimacing and howling like I was lifting 3 human beings. It was intense. My ego was shattered. I was way out of my comfort zone.

But I was sure of one thing. I would lift 100. It didn't matter how long it took. I would do it. That became the goal I set for myself. It's not clear how I arrived at it, but there it was, refusing to dissipate in importance. I went hard. I injured myself. I didn't eat enough. I ate too much. It was very confounding.

Needless to say, my progress wasn't linear. But I had visualised it. It was within my gift. I knew it was within my reach. I didn't doubt it for a second. I just had to prep for it. There were days when the world thought I had lost the plot. The calluses on my hands would be bleeding. My back would be sore, stiff and tight. My big toes would be over-strained. There were moments when I thought I couldn't go on, especially when the chiropractor would do his thing, crunching my bones and massaging my tight, sore muscles. Oh, the cracks and the debilitating hobble.

I was a dancer – trained to be delicate and light on my feet. And there I was planting my toes to ensure they didn't move, at all. The doubting, the double guessing. I wasn't meant to be a strong woman. Oh, the anguish of bones of the constant doubting. In that instance, I would question everything. And yet I would be at the gym the next day, building for my 100.

It was hard. Every time the weights moved up, it was almost like I was lifted on the wings of hope and faith.

I would fly home to talk about it. My family rooted for me. They saw the sparkle in my eyes. It helped that my hugely talented coach was equally resolute. He built new pathways for me. The only way was up. It was going to happen.

Christmas holidays - December 2020, I conquered 70 kilos. And I jumped for joy. That day was fabulous.

I was one of the few women in the gym who lifted and aspired to lift heavy. Everyone cheered. We were a team. It was alive. The game was on. I was physically and mentally gunning for 100 kilos. They were gunning for my success. Gym buddies and gym bros are a fabulous bunch of people!

My well-wishers wondered why I was putting myself through this unknown quantity of pain. Let's not mince words. There is pain. There is pain and agony. Nobody they knew, men or women, had ever attempted to lift 100 kilos. It was unheard of. They were ok with the calluses on my feet from hours and hours of dancing. But this was entirely out of syllabus.

My sister was beginning to get worried. My husband encouraged me to lift safely, especially as he had to deal with the aftermath of my sessions.

But the unknown upside of all this was my daughter is now sees how normal it is for women to lift and be strong – physically and mentally—a massive upside. I wouldn't trade it for anything in the world.

We had trained through everything to lift 100 kilos. Rain, shine, work pressures and the global pandemic notwithstanding. In March 2022, I lifted 90 kilos. I was ecstatic. I over-imagined my strength and underestimated the training requirements. I loaded my 100, but it wouldn't give.

I bowed deeply to the rack and walked away. I knew better. I had learnt the hard way. I wasn't going to push through this one. It needed more build. I needed to be patient and sincere in my training. It was almost there. My universe cheered me on. My work buddies rooted for me.

It was July 2022, a couple of days before my birthday. I was flying solo at the gym and had loaded my weights. They kept flying. And just like that, I loaded my 100 - a 166% over my body weight. I worked through my setup, braced, said a little prayer, and screamed the key word in my head. UP.

In a matter of a few seconds, I had lifted 100 kilos and stared at myself in the mirror and a giant grimace stared back at me. Resolute and stone willed. And it hit me! My 100 kilos. In my grip. Literally. Veni, vidi, vici. Swift and decisive. A 100. Mission complete. The gym erupted. Unloaded, re-racked, bowed to the rack and flew home to tell my people! I will not forget the tiny victory dance we did – round and round. Mummy had done it. She had lifted a 100 kilos!

I was now the only person we knew in our circles (doesn't include my gym buddies and Instagram influencers) to have attempted and lifted 100 kilos. I was elated and grateful in equal measures.

Thrilled to have been able to be on this journey. Grateful to everyone who contributed to the possibility. Immensely happy to find new muscles. Pun intended.

In hindsight, always a privilege; you need a few sharp ones in your toolkit to smile through life. So I thought I would write it here and share it with anyone who needed a lift.

But fundamental to everything – you must articulate your ambitions to achieve your goals, your dream. Find your people. You are going to need expert coaching. Listen to them. They are on your side. They are in your corner. Feed your faith and build. It is not a sprint. It is a triathlon.

A few ideas :

Visualise. It's important to know what you are building for. Visualise. In any way that seems natural for you. Pen, sketch, doodle. Do what you need to do. But have a fair idea of what you are looking to create. But also allow the creative process to create new paths and offshoots and take you where you didn't imagine you could or would.

Prepare well. There are no shortcuts. This one is a bit hard. But you need to build muscle memory. You need to work through the kinks. You need to work on form and technique. You must have your basics in place or risk letting your team down. Remember, a team is as strong as its weakest link.

Pray hard. We always begin with offering prayers to the Maker of the Universe, the guru (teacher) and our parents and finally, to the audience. It's the holy trinity of the stage. Humility is key. Stakeholder management is fundamental. Performance metrics and success are the total of all experiences – manager, colleagues, peers and your team. It is imperative to carry everyone along for the ride.

Smile and wave. Everyone is human and to err is just par for the course. It will happen. Murphy will appear. You can hope for the best and prep for the worst. Go extempore. Remember, no one else can tell the difference between what was planned painstakingly versus a quick fix. But what everyone will remember is how you handled it. It's crucial to look Murphy in the eye and say, "Let's dance."

Upskill, constantly. Find new ground to dance on. Wakeboarding, Hacking, Knitting or Lifting. You define your new ground. You pick your weapons of choice. You pick your new avatar.

ABOUT THE AUTHOR

DIVYA ANAND

Divya Anand is a change maker. She is a passionate and purpose driven strategist and marketeer.

Having lived and worked across India, Thailand, Sri Lanka and Singapore, she has built and solved for the corporate mandate across sectors, organisations and cultures.

In addition to driving the reputation mandate, she is also responsible for enabling the regional revenue growth imperative in her current role.

Divya is also an Indian classical dancer and works with children in her free time to enable effective communication, using dance as a medium.

You can connect with Divya at:

✉ : divyame.anand@gmail.com

in : https://www.linkedin.com/in/divya-anand/

Raising Your Voice

We all have an opinion, a view or simply, thoughts about things that happen to or around us. Some think, some speak, but the majority do nothing.

But what if you are the one who does something about it and takes charge of a situation, turning challenges into inspiration? Don't you want to be heard and even help those who don't dare to speak? Well, we want to hear from you!

At **GLOBAL INFLUENCERS PUBLISHING HOUSE,** we publish books that inspire, motivate, empower, teach, enrich, connect, inform, stimulate or simply make you laugh.

OUR OBJECTIVE is to connect the hearts and minds of our international readers and authors through the power of words. **THE TEAM** who work behind the scenes, around the clock, making all this magic happen, have been handpicked for their skill, talent, dedication and passion for achieving our objective.

So, if you have a **STORY** to share, send us a message on: **shikha@globalinfluencers.sg**

You can also join the **#MY VOICE FORUM**, which provides a network for like-minded women worldwide to come together to talk about things that matter. A safe space where we can agree, disagree, or agree to disagree but without any judgement, discuss issues and challenges faced, lend a listening ear or a helping hand to one another, find solutions and ultimately take action to make change happen.

To find out more, go to: www.facebook.com/groups/myvoiceforum

"Together we will embark on a new journey by creating the world we deserve to live in."

- Neera Gupta,

Chief Visionary Officer at

Global Influencers Publishing House.

Made in the USA
Middletown, DE
03 April 2023

27633102R00146